Staying Sober Without God

The Practical 12 Steps to Long-Term Recovery from Alcoholism and Addictions

Jeffrey Munn, LMFT

ISBN-13: 978-1-7335880-0-3

DEDICATION

This book is dedicated to my amazing wife, Rose, whose love and support was instrumental in my ability to complete this project while juggling school, work, and family life.

And to my daughter, Averie. You are a beautiful human being and an endless source of joy and love in my life. Daddy loves you.

WORKBOOK AVAILABLE ON AMAZON!

Visit www.practicallysane.org for more info, blogs, and private coaching. Sign up for the mailing list to receive the latest news and updates.

CONTENTS

ACKNOWLEDGMENTS

Thanks to everyone who has helped me on my personal journey in recovery. To Oscar, sponsor #34 (roughly) who taught me how to approach the steps in a way that didn't require belief in the supernatural. You gave me guidance, compassion, and a couch to sleep on when I was at my lowest.

To Robert Crane, hearing a successful author tell me that this was possible was more life-changing than you realize. The seed you planted has grown into confidence, excitement, and the book you currently hold in your hand. Your support and encouragement has meant so much.

To my parents, without whom I wouldn't exist. At least, that's how I've been told it works. Thanks for always believing in me and supporting my endeavors in the field of mental health.

Last but not least, thank you to all my clients. This book would not exist without you. Your incredible bravery and willingness to engage in the process of self-development inspires me on a daily basis. You give me the drive and motivation to be the best therapist and teacher that I can be.

The Practical 12 Steps

1. Admitted we were caught in a self-destructive cycle and currently lacked the tools to stop it

2. Trusted that a healthy lifestyle was attainable through social support and consistent self-improvement

3. Committed to a lifestyle of recovery, focusing only on what we could control

4. Made a comprehensive list of our resentments, fears, and harmful actions

5. Shared our lists with a trustworthy person

6. Made a list of our unhealthy character traits

7. Began cultivating healthy character traits through consistent positive behavior

8. Determined the best way to make amends to those we had harmed

9. Made direct amends to such people wherever possible, except when to do so would cause harm

10. Practiced daily self-reflection and continued making amends whenever necessary

11. We started meditating

12. Sought to retain our newfound recovery lifestyle by teaching it to those willing to learn and by surrounding ourselves with healthy people

CHAPTER ONE
INTRODUCTION

I first got clean and sober when I was 20 years old. I hit rock bottom very early in life thanks to the fact that I was a phenomenally low-functioning addict. Other than consuming just enough food to survive and shuffling to the restroom, nothing took priority over my addiction. The only time I stopped obsessing about getting high was in the first few moments after getting high. Shortly thereafter, my buzz would start to wear off and the obsession would resume. Thankfully, the people in my life did not enable me for long. I was eventually left with the choice to get sober or waste away until I was either locked up, homeless, or dead.

My first 12-step meeting was not the typical experience for a newcomer. I actually enjoyed it immensely and instantly felt at home. I started attending meetings often and quickly saw some improvements in my life. I had some new relationships, a few healthier habits, and a glimmer of hope that I could possibly live a happy, productive life. The only thing that nagged at me was the constant talk of God. He was mentioned by some name or another in half of the steps and nearly every member had brought him up at some point while sharing during the meetings. I had been more or less an agnostic since about the age of seven, but I had such an overall positive experience in the first meetings that I was willing to check my beliefs at the door and try something new. And try I did.

I sought guidance about the "God thing" from my sponsor[1] and other 12-step members over the course of the next few years. I was told to begin searching for a "God of my understanding." I tried every suggestion that was thrown at me, from writing a list of my ideal God's character traits to praying first thing every morning. I was consistently promised that if I sought God, he would eventually start to have an impact on my life. I was told that if I wasn't noticing his effect on my life, it was because I either wasn't looking hard enough or because I was subconsciously discounting the evidence. "Have you used drugs or alcohol today?", I would be asked. "No," I'd respond, only to then be told, "That is God working in your life!"

Was it really God? Was it really a supernatural being that listened to my prayers and made subtle changes to my mental state and the events in my life so that I could remain sober? How can anyone say for sure that God was the reason for these changes? And why is it that these changes all look strikingly similar to changes that would probably occur anyway if someone engaged in consistent, mindful, healthy behavior? These questions plagued me early in recovery. I attempted to find ways around the concept of God. I tried working with very vague definitions of a "higher power," but that never felt genuine. Eventually, the persistent message that recovery was impossible without a supernatural, intervening God wore me down. So I stopped going to meetings.

During the first few weeks after I stopped going to meetings, I felt pretty good. I felt free from the expectations of the program and its members. I felt like a regular guy again. I spent time with non-addicts, went to parties, went to bars, and just tried really hard (i.e. "white knuckling") not to drink or use. That worked pretty well for me for a while. Unfortunately, I began to feel left out. I grew resentful of my sobriety and the fact that drugs and alcohol affected me differently than they affected others. I felt entitled to a "normal" life where I could indulge once in a while. My anxiety and depressive symptoms resurfaced as I was faced with life challenges that I no longer had the tools or support to face. After about a month of my discomfort becoming increasingly worse, I decided a beer was a good idea.

I relapsed after two and a half years sober. It didn't take long for me to end up as desperate and alone as I was before. Within the first day of my relapse, I was lying to my loved ones, sneaking around, and keeping secrets. I quickly came to the conclusion that I had to get back into recovery. I knew I'd probably go back to meetings, but this time I would go for the social support and instead seek my mental and emotional growth through psychotherapy. Die-hard 12-steppers would tell me that seeking long-term sobriety through anything other than a spiritual awakening through God was a recipe for failure. Regardless, I did what felt right for me.

I attended an inpatient treatment facility where I worked with a number of incredibly passionate and well-trained therapists. Nowhere was there a mention of God. Instead, we discussed childhood trauma, grief and loss, personal responsibility, relationship patterns, emotional intelligence, healthy communication, and mindfulness. I had so many realizations and epiphanies during my brief 45-day stay at rehab that I left feeling like a different human being. I suddenly understood things about myself and the world that I never learned growing up. This powerful experience of self-discovery had a huge impact on my life and led me to want to become a psychotherapist myself.

Shortly after leaving inpatient treatment, I enrolled in graduate school to earn my master's degree in clinical psychology. I had the unique experience of learning about theories of psychotherapy while also being part of the 12-step community. Over time, I began to see that the spiritual and religious experiences that people were having in the 12-step program could make just as much—if not more—sense from a psychological perspective. I also discovered how to have these experiences myself, with no supernatural belief required.

If you're reading this book, chances are you've already had some experience with the 12-step world in one or more of its many manifestations. Perhaps you've attended a meeting of Alcoholics Anonymous, Narcotics Anonymous, Overeaters Anonymous, Gamblers Anonymous, Sex Addicts Anonymous, Al-Anon, or any of the other countless programs that have emerged since the initial founding of AA. While all of these programs focus on different behaviors, the 12 steps are the common thread that connects them all.

I'm going to also assume that you're reading this book because you've looked at the steps or perhaps even attempted to work through them, yet, like myself, had a less-than-warm reaction to seeing the word "God" in there. Maybe you were even open to the idea of God or a higher power at first, but it never felt quite right when you tried to incorporate it into your life. Regardless of whether you came into the program as a non-believer, became one later on, or are still on the fence, you've decided to see if a secular approach to the 12 steps is possible. Spoiler alert: it is.

I have spent many years in 12-step programs. I've worked with addicts, alcoholics, and codependents of all types in both the 12-step world and in my work as a psychotherapist. There is no doubt that faith and spirituality can play a tremendous role in the recovery of many people, but I have come to believe that it is not only unnecessary, but potentially harmful when imposed on recovering addicts for whom a faith-based approach is not a good fit.

Over the years, I've witnessed far too many desperate addicts feel pressured to shoehorn the concept of God into their recovery, only to end up feeling discouraged and frustrated when it doesn't provide the results they were told to expect. Upon telling their fellows that their attempts to connect with a god hasn't worked, they are led to believe they are doing something wrong or that they're overanalyzing and are "too smart for their own good."

This book is not intended to bash those who have a concept of God that works for them. It is intended for the men and women seeking help who have been led to believe that there is no place for them in the 12-step community if they don't believe in the supernatural. It's for the people who have been told their use of logic and reason is "stinking thinking" and that they need to ignore their own instincts. It's for those who see the benefits of the 12 step meetings and programs, but don't know how to reconcile their need for support with their lack of belief in God.

Logic and reason are skills that you can learn to improve; they enhance your recovery rather than hinder it. The commonly-used slogan, "My best thinking got me here" is one of the most potentially damaging phrases I hear repeated in 12-step meetings. It's a phrase that implies that we are fundamentally incapable of effectively using our own thinking to navigate through life. Our best thinking doesn't destroy our lives, our worst thinking does. Recovery is the process of improving your thinking, changing your lifestyle, and trusting that you have the ability to live a rich, full life without engaging in life-crushing compulsive behaviors.

I've meant for this book to be read through from beginning to end, but it can also be used as a reference. You can skip around to specific areas of the book as you need them without missing anything too critical. However, if you're looking for more than a secular translation of the 12 steps, I think you'll gain more by reading the entire thing. The beginning of the book will aim to give a general overview of what recovery without God looks like, while the later chapters will focus on each of the 12 steps along with suggested approaches to working through them. After the steps, I will discuss some other recovery tools and principles that I believe the steps don't address adequately.

Regardless of how you choose to work through your steps, I highly suggest doing them with a sponsor instead of by yourself. If you have trouble finding a sponsor who will support a God-free approach to the steps (there are more out there than you realize), you can still work the God-full version with him or her and use this book to help you view some of the more supernatural-sounding concepts through a rational lens. I believe there is a down-to-earth, logical counterpart to every spiritual principle taught through the 12 steps, and with a little critical thinking and guidance from this book, my hope is that you'll be able to interpret the program in a way that makes sense to you.

It's my belief that these steps can help anyone, not just addicts. For the purpose of this book, however, my discussion of recovery will focus on recovery from substance addiction, codependency, and behavioral addictions such as gambling and sex. Can you use these steps if you're just trying to watch less TV or become a generally healthier person? Sure. This process can help you improve any area of your life. If you want a book dedicated to a broader use of the 12 steps, however, this isn't that. It certainly can still help you, but some of the information about addiction may not pertain to you.

I do not claim to be the authority on recovery for atheists and agnostics. This book is simply my point of view as a long-time sober addict and mental health professional who has worked with many individuals struggling with addictive behaviors. Ultimately, I am a fan of what works. If this book doesn't speak to you, please continue searching until you find an approach to recovery that suits your specific needs.

Who is God, Anyway?

Throughout this guide, I will regularly use the word "God." If you ask a hundred people what God means or who he is, you'll get a hundred different answers. For the purposes of this book, I define God as any supernatural being or force that is capable of directly intervening in your life. I am not including some of the more nebulous definitions of God that I've run across over the years, such as:

- God is any force, real or imagined, that keeps you sober.
- God is the combined love and support of the 12-step group members.
- God is the universe.
- God is a higher state of mind.
- God is not a being, but a set of actions.
- God can be anything, even a doorknob.

Yes, the doorknob one is real. People say that. If you've noticed significant changes in your life as a result of praying to a piece of hardware, I'd encourage you to continue. As I said before, I'm a fan of whatever works. In fact, if *any* one of the above definitions of God works for you, please continue embracing it. If you're reading this, however, chances are you need something more concrete.

There is no one thing that is an adequate replacement for the concept of God. The word "God" is used in the 12-step world to refer to a multitude of different experiences, phenomena, and concepts. While I will attempt to keep my approach as simple as possible, I should stress that real life tends to be more complex than belief in the supernatural. If working the 12 steps without God was as simple as replacing the word with something like "love" or "wisdom," there wouldn't be so many people struggling with it.

A brief side note on grammar: I do not capitalize "God" for any reason other than grammatical accuracy. I capitalize "God" because it is a proper noun and it should be capitalized just as one would capitalize "Robert" or "Paris." When I don't capitalize the word "God," it's because I'm using the word as a common noun, such as in the phrase, "Odin is a god." I personally prefer Thor.

Is There a Substitute for Religious Faith?

Like I said, there's no *one* thing that seems to be a sufficient replacement for faith in God. It seems hard to deny that placing faith in a benevolent supreme being or religion does provide a unique sense of comfort and meaning to those who are capable of doing so. So what is happening for them, and how can we replicate these effects for ourselves without engaging in an act of faith? If we go by the assumption that a supernatural force isn't at play, then there must be something psychological occurring to people of faith. In this section, we'll take a look at some of the changes that faith in a god or higher power can bring about and then explore what can fulfill the same role for nonbelievers.

One of the most notable psychological changes that occurs when someone places their faith in a supreme being is that they no longer feel the need to try and control everything. They are able to let go of how the world responds to their actions and focus only on the actions themselves. They feel cared for and watched over. This practice of "letting go and letting God" is very powerful. The only difference for us atheists and agnostics is that we are leaving out the "letting God" part. Instead, we just practice letting go and letting the rest unfold as it may. Rather than believing a supernatural being is behind the scenes pulling strings and moving chess pieces, we simply acknowledge that there is a complicated world out there that is going to do what it does whether we like it or not. Coming to this realization eases our burden and helps us stop worrying, micromanaging, and manipulating others. We are able to do our part and accept whatever the results are (what religious folk would call "God's will"). We may not feel as cared for as those who believe in God, but I consider this a positive thing because it pushes us to take a more active role in caring for ourselves.

In addition to letting go of control, those who place their faith in a supreme being also feel a connection to something much bigger than themselves. The result is a sense of purpose and meaning, which is an important ingredient for cultivating confidence, motivation, and joy in our lives. While believing in God works for some, what options do non-believers have to achieve the same experience? The answer is different depending on what you are drawn to. Some, like myself, can derive a sense of awe, wonder, and meaning just from contemplating the cosmos and our existence within it, as well as the process of evolution that made us what we are today.

The universe and everything it is composed of is so mind-bendingly vast and complex that I find it impossible to think about without feeling a profound and often euphoric sense of wonder and meaning. Some might even call this a "spiritual" experience. I choose to think of it as a natural result of exploring the reality of our reality. You may not have the same experience when contemplating the universe. It can cause some people to feel small and insignificant, which is the opposite of what we're going for. If that's your case, you can still find something more down-to-earth to feel connected to, such as nature, humanity, or even a specific community.

And finally, faith in a religion or belief system gives people a specific set of instructions and guiding principles for life. The power of this is that it relieves us of the pressure of needing to figure everything out on our own. Our inherent human need for a blueprint for living life is why we often see people take to certain causes or lifestyles such as dietary lifestyles, political beliefs, fitness trends, and humanitarian causes similarly to how some take to religion. Having a focus and direction in life is an important part of our identity and necessary for us to feel competent and valuable. The problem with getting our guidance from dogmatic belief systems like religion or traditional 12-step approaches is that the wisdom is often dated and doesn't evolve much over time. These belief systems tend to be rigid and don't allow for questioning or critical thinking.

Atheists and agnostics still have a need for direction and purpose, but how do we obtain this without subscribing to a dogma? Hopefully, this book will help serve that function. However, just as I don't believe that any one religious doctrine provides all the answers, nor do I believe anyone should live their entire life according to one self-help book. That would be restricting your natural ability to grow and evolve as a human being. As time goes on, our world changes, and so do we. Rather than having a set-in-stone guide for living, we should all strive to stick to some basic guiding principles while continuing to explore and grow in other aspects of our life as we learn more about ourselves and our place in the world. The truth is, the basic foundation for living a happy life consists of a small number of basic principles. The rest is for us to figure out and fine-tune as we gain life experience.

Most of the principles that I believe are crucial for living a healthy life are outlined throughout this book. My experience has been that living according to these principles and practicing these behaviors can provide us with everything that religious faith does and more. Ultimately, however, I don't want you to take my word for anything written in here. Instead, in the spirit of being self-sufficient and finding your own way, just give the ideas and exercises here a try and decide for yourself if they work for you.

CHAPTER TWO
WHAT IS ADDICTION?

Some folk in recovery will have you believe that addiction is a relatively simple thing. It is sometimes referred to as a "two-fold disease," being an "obsession of the mind coupled with an allergy of the body." Sometimes it's simply thought of as a spiritual malady, implying that an intangible, invisible, immeasurable force within you is somehow capable of contracting a condition that affects your mental health. Needless to say, I believe these conceptions fall tragically short of reality, and while I don't think understanding addiction is necessary in order to recover from it, I reckon it does help.

At its core, addiction is the experience of not being able to stop using a substance or engaging in a behavior despite a genuine desire to stop. People generally discover that they are addicts after they have tried several times to stop or moderate their behavior, only to be repeatedly frustrated by failure. Sometimes, there may be periods of success. For example, a daily drinker may swear off alcohol and go for a few days, weeks, or even months without it. Eventually, however, without major fundamental changes to their lifestyle, they slide back into old patterns and the cycle begins again.

Addiction is the combination of being in a state of emotional discomfort (often discomfort we are not consciously aware of) and having a previous experience with a powerfully soothing substance or behavior. We've learned that this substance or behavior works, so we engage in it whenever we feel the need for relief, which can be practically constant if we haven't dealt with the root cause. To make matters worse, our underlying discomfort increases as a result of this cycle, making us seek even more relief. To put it really simply, we feel crummy, so we crave relief. We know that [insert drug or behavior here] makes us feel better, so we do it whenever we want to feel better, which can be all the time. It stops working as effectively as it did at first, so we do it more or move on to other things that have a stronger effect. In the case of substances, we also can develop a physical dependence, which complicates things further. The drug or behavior becomes so essential to our comfort that we can't muster the willingness to stop without help. We are addicted.

It's important to understand that addiction, like most things, exists on a spectrum. Some people have a much harder time controlling their addictive behaviors than others. Some need intensive treatment and some seem to be able to do it with minimal assistance. It's not black or white. If you've had the experience of not being able to fully control a behavior despite wanting to, then congratulations, you're part of the club. You've experienced addiction and can probably benefit from the tools of recovery. Don't compare yourself to other people with addiction, compare yourself to yesterday's version of yourself.

People will sometimes argue that a particular behavior or substance is "not addictive," and therefore impossible to get addicted to. For example, you may hear that marijuana is not addictive or that sex addiction isn't real. As far as I'm concerned, if you have tried to stop or moderate your marijuana use and can't seem to, you fall somewhere on the marijuana addiction spectrum. If you've engaged in compulsive sexual behavior despite attempts not to, you fall somewhere on the sex addiction spectrum. Don't listen to the arbitrary rules that others make up about addiction. Look honestly at *your* experience. That's all that matters.

That's not to say that certain substances aren't more prone to trigger addiction than others. That is certainly true, but don't confuse that with the idea that there is any pleasurable psychoactive drug or pleasurable behavior that is completely excluded from the list of possible addictions. And even though there may be drugs such as heroin or meth that are more prone to trigger addiction, there are significant variations from person to person. Cocaine may *usually* trigger addiction more severely than marijuana, but I've encountered a few cases in which the addict compulsively smoked weed and hated their experiences with cocaine. Addiction is highly dependent on your individual response to any given pleasurable activity.

Will I Always Be an Addict?

Yes. Well, probably. I mean, we don't actually know for sure. The signs seem to point to the likelihood that most people who experience an addiction will likely struggle to some extent in that area for the rest of their lives. Some people may improve, and in other cases they may get worse over time, even if they aren't actively using. Some research suggests that, once a person becomes sensitized to a substance, there are permanent changes that occur in the brain that do not seem to reverse fully over time[2]. The bottom line is that we are short on conclusive information in this area and more studies need to be conducted before we can say with any kind of certainty how a person's tendency toward addiction can change over time. If you ask the opinion of most addiction professionals, they will probably tell you that going back to drinking or using responsibly is a pipe dream, and I tend to agree.

The answer to this question is much more complicated when it comes to behavioral addictions, however. Some research suggests that behavioral addictions or compulsions operate very similarly to substance addictions, while some research shows them to be more similar to obsessive-compulsive disorder[3]. In other words, we're not even sure it's the same "type" of addiction that occurs with drugs and alcohol. Most behavioral addicts will report a loss of control that is nearly identical to alcoholism or drug addiction. They can't seem to control their behavior despite the fact that it has resulted in significant negative consequences.

The biggest challenge when treating some of these behavioral addictions is that the behaviors themselves are necessary on some level in order to fulfill our basic needs (such as eating or having sex). In other words, addicts *must* learn to control their addiction. It takes a very detailed, specific plan that restricts certain behaviors and allows others. Now, you may be thinking, "If behavioral addicts can learn to moderate their addiction, doesn't that mean alcoholics could learn to drink alcohol normally?" It's a fair question, but I think there are some key differences between substance addiction and behavioral addictions that make that a weak argument, and since it's beyond the scope of this book, I'll save that discussion for another time.

Am I saying it's impossible to go from addict to non-addict? No. As you've probably realized, I (almost) never like to speak in absolutes. That being said, I have not seen any convincing instances of people with serious addictions becoming completely non-compulsive. I've heard anecdotal reports from others, but it's not scientifically sound to base a conclusion on stories alone. With our current knowledge of the subject, I will say that, even if it's possible, it's pretty unlikely and probably not worth the risk. If you are convinced that you will one day be able to fully control a substance you used to be addicted to, then I won't stop you from trying. If you're successful, please share your story with me. If you aren't, there's always a spot for you in the recovery world.

CHAPTER THREE
RECOVERING WITHOUT GOD

What is Recovery?

Before we start getting into the secular approach to recovery, it's probably a good idea to talk about what the term "recovery" even means. As far as this book goes, "recovery" is defined as the life-long process of improving your overall mental and emotional health so as to minimize the harm and suffering you inflict on yourself and others. While the goal for many of you is likely to stay sober, I want to emphasize that the absence of destructive behaviors is just one point on an otherwise endless journey of self-improvement. If all you care about is not using, these methods can get you there, but just know that they can continue to benefit you for the rest of your time on Earth, far beyond just achieving a state of not wanting to get high.

Recovery is not an event or a finite process; it's a lifestyle. It requires fundamental changes to be made to the way you look at and interact with the world and the people in it. Knowing this, it's understandable to see why so many people think that a drastic spiritual experience is a necessary part of recovery. A spiritual awakening usually changes a person's priorities, self-image, and beliefs about the world in one fell swoop. Unfortunately, such spiritual experiences often require an act of faith, and even people capable of such acts of faith don't often experience the "white light" spiritual awakenings that create big change in a short amount of time.

More often, this type of transformative experience takes place slowly as one continues to make small, incremental steps towards improving themselves. It often starts through interaction with healthy people, which is why meetings have a lot to offer. That being said, you can certainly start this work on your own. All it takes is a willingness to try something new and make a small effort every day to engage in new habits and behaviors. Though I believe the 12 steps leave some important things out, they are actually a great place to start, which is why I base this book on them. In the following chapter, I will explain the basic purpose of each of the 12 steps along with the principles that make them effective.

Will I Fully Recover or Will I Always Be Recovering?

If I had a dollar for every time I heard 12-step members arguing about this, I'd have a fair amount of dollars. I've overheard (and been involved in) a few arguments about whether recovery is a life-long process or a finite process that we can finish. Some will insist that recovery never ends, while some will tell you that working the steps will get you fully recovered. As you might have guessed, the answer to this question is not so black-and-white. The members of AA who state that we can fully recover are referring to recovering from what is described in the Big Book of Alcoholics Anonymous as "a hopeless state of mind and body." The members of AA who state that recovery is everlasting are referring to the fact that we are constantly striving towards abstract ideals that we will never achieve perfectly.

If you think about it, both of these things can be true. We can get to a point in our recovery where we are no longer experiencing certain kinds of suffering, in which case it makes sense to say we've recovered from a certain state of mind. We can also never get to a place in our life where we have achieved perfection and have no more room for improvement, in which case it makes sense to say we will always be recovering. The argument of recovered vs. recovering is an unnecessary source of disagreement in the program. We can recover, and we will always be recovering. It's not as complicated as some people make it out to be, so don't get caught up on it.

Why the 12 Steps?

You may be wondering why I would choose to stick with a 12-step format rather than just creating my own program from scratch. Despite the problems with 12-step programs and some of the messages in the meetings, the original 12 steps actually have a lot of wisdom in them. The truth is that very few of the ideas outlined in the 12 steps were genuinely new ideas at the time. Many of them were adapted from a group known as The Oxford Group. The steps even share some very common-sense principles with the eightfold path in Buddhism. The psychological and "spiritual" concepts that evolved into the 12 steps have lasted for as long as they have because there is something in them that works. While the religious and supernatural aspects of the 12 steps are not a good fit for many, it's important not to throw the proverbial baby out with the bathwater. If you're able to look past the less desirable stuff, you'll see there's quite a bit of material in the original 12 steps that makes practical sense.

The basic path of the steps goes something like this: you start with admitting you have an issue that needs fixing. Afterwards, you accept that you can't fix it all by yourself. You then commit to seeking outside help. Once you do that, you begin doing some inner work, starting with looking at all your resentments, fears, and guilt. You confess these to someone you trust, who then helps you look at what personal qualities enable you to engage in these unhealthy behaviors. The undesirable qualities are listed, and you make efforts to be rid of them. After you've made peace with yourself, you then make amends to those you've hurt. You maintain the results of this process by engaging in regular maintenance behaviors like meditation, self-reflection, and service.

That doesn't sound so crazy, does it? The foundation of the classic 12 steps is fairly solid. There's a reason it seems to have helped so many people. Unfortunately, it comes with so much baggage that it turns a lot of people away. In addition to that, it frames some of the changes it creates in a way that is disempowering rather than empowering. The wording of the steps often leads to people believing that all good things in their lives are a result of God, and all (or most) bad things are a result of them not being in line with God's will for them. It's not uncommon for people to grow resentful of this message and rebel against it, and I don't particularly blame them.

Staying Sober Without God is an approach to the 12 steps that empowers the individual, reframes spiritual changes as real-world psychological events, and adds a few concrete actions that can aid in the lifestyle and personality changes needed to bring about lasting recovery. They are devoid of anything outside the realm of the natural world. Rather than requiring the help of the supposed creator of the universe, we are building confidence in our own ability to rewire our brains, establish new behavior patterns, and make the choice to live a better life.

CHAPTER FOUR
THE PRACTICAL 12 STEPS

The following chapter consists of 12 sections, each one dedicated to the practical adaptation of the original 12 steps of Alcoholics Anonymous. I will offer my description of the step followed by an explanation of how it fits into a recovery lifestyle. Some of the original steps that don't deal with God will get some fine-tuning, while the steps that are God-heavy will get a major overhaul. At the end of each chapter, I will suggest various ways to "work" these steps. If you or your sponsor can think of other ways that suit your individual style better, then by all means, try them. You may love expressing yourself through art. I'm not an art therapist, so I don't make a lot of specific suggestions related to art. That doesn't mean it's any worse or better than any other approach. Everyone has an approach that works for them. Find yours.

You may have seen non-theistic versions of the 12 steps other places on the internet, but the aim of my Practical 12 Steps is to provide more than just an irreligious translation of the steps. My goal is to provide a comprehensive guide to working these steps that offers the same kind of growth and self-discovery that the traditional 12 steps offer to theistic members of the recovery world. It's also important to note that not all steps mention God. Even so, I have still adapted them in order to create a fully revamped and thorough program. Some of the changes that I've made to the wording of the steps change core concepts, while other changes I've made are just for the sake of clarity and simplicity.

The language in the original 12 steps can sometimes be vague. For example, turning "your will and your life over to the care of God" has lots of different meanings to different people. Even with the instructions offered in the Big Book of Alcoholics Anonymous and its accompanying literature, it's often challenging for anyone (especially newcomers) to develop a full understanding of what the step is asking them to do. My goal for the Practical 12 Steps is to be as clear and concrete as possible. I'm aiming for language that leaves little-to-no room for misinterpretation. That being said, most written work is open to several interpretations, so if you have any questions, feel free to send me an email or discuss any confusion with your sponsor or therapist. At the end of the day, giving these steps a genuine effort is more important than understanding them perfectly.

If you're reading this book solely for information and are not currently working the steps, you may feel the desire to skip the "working the step" section after each step. However, reading it may still provide you with some good information regardless of whether you are planning on working them or not. The sections detailing how to work each step contain more than dry instructions and often expand upon information from the previous section. The choice is still up to you (I'm all about empowerment, remember?).

When Am I Done with a Step?

Some of the steps have very clear and definite endings, while most of them do not. Early in recovery, I often nagged my sponsor about when I could move on to the next step—kind of a twitchy addict version of, "are we there yet?" He would often respond with a vague answer like, "let's just be *in* this step for a bit longer." This answer made me grumpy, but I understand it now that I've perfected the art of recovery (I haven't). While it can be tempting to work through these steps quickly and efficiently, that isn't always the best choice.

All of these steps require a certain level of patience and introspection. Rushing through them might limit their effectiveness. Steps such as step six, which directs you to make a list of unhealthy character traits, will be best accomplished slowly and thoroughly. That's not to say you need to spend a month on each step, but you should do your best to be honest with yourself about how completely you feel you've accomplished each task. If you're comfortable that you've done your best, and your sponsor or guide agrees, then go ahead and move on. Don't obsess about getting it perfect. Step nine, for example, guides you to make amends to the people that you've harmed, but you don't have to refrain from moving on to step ten until every single amends on your list is complete. Do what you are reasonably able to given your current resources. If you can honestly say to yourself that you've given it your best, then it's fine to move forward and revisit the step later if you feel the need to.

Important Considerations Before Beginning the Steps

It's important to understand that, while these steps are powerful and potentially very useful, they are not the only answer, nor are they a complete treatment program in and of themselves. I have designed these steps to go a bit deeper than the original steps, but that does not mean they will magically solve any issue that you have. Sometimes, more actions need to be taken in order to achieve a state of stability and move towards optimal mental health. Mental health is ultimately very complex and is influenced by countless factors in our lives. It has been studied for centuries and we are still barely scratching the surface of understanding why people do what they do or feel how they feel. For that reason, there is simply no way to develop a cookie-cutter approach that will completely "fix" someone. These steps can help a lot, but they are not the be-all and end-all.

Some of the younger members of the 12-step world are catching on to the fact that these steps are not a panacea. Even so, it's common to hear the steps presented in meetings as a system that can be applied to any problem in life. I strongly disagree with this. Not only have extreme versions of the 12-steps-cures-all approach (such as The Pacific Group) caused harm, they have legitimately ruined lives and resulted in the deaths of vulnerable people. While it's true that some people can receive the bulk of their recovery from the program, I believe there are things the program misses (which I'll get into in later chapters) that are necessary for a well-rounded, healthy life in recovery. I encourage you to never close your mind off to other tools you can add to your life that may enhance your recovery, and if you feel pressure from anyone in or out of the program to avoid getting outside help, run away from that person as quickly as possible.

Mental Health

I'm going to say this multiple times throughout this book because it is *so important.* I cannot stress this enough. I think *everyone* who is attempting to get sober should also be thoroughly assessed by a mental health professional. Ideally, this would be a master's level clinician such as an LPCC, MFT, or LCSW, or a doctorate-level clinician such as a psychologist (PsyD or PhD). Psychiatrists are medical doctors and are also an option, but I suggest you ask around and find someone who does very thorough assessments and has some experience doing talk therapy. It's even better if they have a background in addiction. There are many psychiatrists out there who simply talk to patients for 10-20 minutes and prescribe medication. I do not believe that to be sufficient.

Mental health is no joke. If you are struggling with severe anxiety, panic, major depression, PTSD, unresolved grief or trauma, OCD, delusional disorders, bipolar disorder, or any number of other mental health conditions, you *absolutely must* see a mental health professional. There is no substitute for this. These steps are not a cure for mental health problems. They are part of a balanced recovery breakfast for people who want to improve their lives and reduce their desire to engage in self-destructive behaviors. They can absolutely be done as a complement to professional therapy if you want, but they should *never* be used as a replacement for professional help.

If you have insurance, I highly suggest reaching out to them and finding a nearby professional who can assess your mental health and provide some psychotherapy if necessary. If you happen to live in a particularly small town or rural area, there are online options such as BetterHelp.com and

Talkspace.com available if necessary, though I always prefer face-to-face. When you go to therapy, do not hold back or keep secrets. You must be honest and open or you will not get the help that you need. If the clinician refers you to other professionals for additional tests or assessments, go. Never let complacency or apathy get in the way of your mental health. You're on this planet once and you only get one brain. Take exceptionally good care of it.

If you don't have insurance, you're going to have a harder time finding help, but that doesn't mean you can't. A few Google searches can potentially find you some sliding-scale or low fee service providers. Sometimes, these providers have fewer qualifications, but they are still likely to be supervised by people with a lot of experience and therefore are far better than not talking to anyone at all. Go to Google and search for "low fee psychotherapy," "affordable therapy," or something similar, and you should be able to find something. If not, call any local therapist and ask them to provide referrals. You're bound to find someone who knows of a place that offers what you need. Often, just the act of seeking therapy can benefit your mental state.

Stopping Your Addictive Behavior

Before we get into any steps, we need to look at abstinence/sobriety. You'll notice that none of the steps ever mention anything about the actual stopping of an addictive behavior. In AA, members stop drinking at various points throughout the program. The story of Dr. Bob, AA's co-founder, states that he didn't get sober until he started making amends to the people he harmed (step nine). He started by going door-to-door around his neighborhood and apologizing to his neighbors, and that was allegedly the last day he ever drank. Some, however, stopped drinking while they were hospitalized before they were even introduced to the steps.

I'm not going to tell you that you have to stop your behavior before working the steps, because sometimes beginning the recovery process is necessary in order to find the strength to stop. That being said, the earlier in the process you stop, the better. If you're actively drinking or using heavy drugs, for example, your perception may be too skewed to properly work the steps. In this case, it may be worth it to do everything you can to completely stop the behavior first, including considering an inpatient detox program, especially if your addiction has brought you to a place where your life is at risk. Things like inpatient rehab or hospitalization may seem huge and scary now, but you will eventually remember them as a small fraction of your overall journey. They can very often be a necessary part of becoming stabilized enough to begin a process such as the one outlined in this book. In addition, if you are addicted to alcohol or benzodiazepines like diazepam (Valium) or alprazolam (Xanax), quitting cold turkey without medical assistance can be fatal. If you're planning to stop, seeking medical help is non-negotiable.

Some addictive behaviors are subtler and less immediately destructive. For example, someone who is trying to stop smoking meth is going to experience very different consequences if they continue than someone who is trying to stop overeating. Abstinence and sobriety will look different depending on what you're trying to change. Some behaviors are quite likely to resurface from time to time throughout the process, while others will be absolutely devastating if you begin engaging in them again. The aim is for complete, sustained abstinence from our addiction, and the importance of hitting that goal is dependent on how destructive our particular addiction is. Someone with a 20-year addiction to alcohol could end up dead if they relapse, while someone who struggles with overeating may slip up and be able to get back on track relatively unscathed. Some addictions are more forgiving than others. It's not fair, but it's the truth. Get honest about how destructive yours is and act accordingly. Speak to a sponsor or mental health professional if you aren't sure what to do.

Attending Meetings

Attending meetings is critically important in early recovery. Is it possible to recover and get sober without them? Sure, it's possible, but I suspect it's far less likely. Social support is often enough to make the difference between sticking with a program and bailing out prematurely. Just as a lifestyle of addiction is powerfully reinforced by being around other addicts, a recovery lifestyle is powerfully reinforced by being around other healthy people in (or out of) recovery[4]. There are few other places in the world where you'll get the opportunity to be surrounded by people who are so willing to talk openly about the same issues you are struggling with. Peer pressure is just as powerful a tool when used for good. It helps to have a group of people who care about you and have an investment in your continued recovery.

Meetings don't have to become your life. Early in recovery, I generally recommend people go to at least three meetings a week. A meeting a day is completely doable, particularly if you are unemployed or without other pressing responsibilities. After a sustained period of sobriety, you can always reevaluate how important meetings are to you. I've known people who swear by meetings and have been going almost daily for decades. I also know people who have not gone to meetings for years and are doing well because they continue to practice their recovery program and surround themselves with people who support their lifestyle. Some people love meetings and some people hate them. What is non-negotiable at any point in your recovery is social support. You absolutely must have a support network. The truth is that *everyone* needs a support network, addict or not. Whether or not this support comes from meetings is moderately important, but not nearly as important as making sure you get it from *somewhere.*

If you can't find meetings that are supportive of your need for a secular approach to the steps, try subbing in some online meetings. There are atheist and agnostic meetings around if you look hard enough. If you can't find these meetings, just go to the regular ones and do your best to listen to the similarities instead of the differences. A lot of the core messages in theist-dominated meetings are similar enough to the ones in this book. The main difference is that this book frames them as psychological and behavioral concepts rather than spiritual or religious ones. Once you've read this book and understand the practical version of the steps, you can fairly easily mentally translate the language used in the more religious 12-step meetings to something that makes more sense to you.

Even in some of the more theistic meetings, you can usually still find someone who is less into the monotheistic, Judeo-Christian, supernatural version of the program. Find these people, get their numbers, and make them part of your support network. The great thing about meetings is you can pick and choose who you decide to stick with and make a part of your life. Recovery is a personal journey and you have to find what works for you. At some point, after you've become a long-timer, you and your Godless heathen friends can even start your own atheist/agnostic meeting for all the other people out there who are looking for the same practical approach you were.

Step One

AA Version

Admitted we were powerless over alcohol—that our lives had become unmanageable

Practical Version

Admitted we were caught in a self-destructive cycle and currently lacked the tools to stop it

The first step is probably the one the general population is most familiar with. It's often paraphrased as, "The first step is admitting you have a problem." That's a decent start, but there's quite a lot more to it. This step consists of two distinct parts. The first part requires us to admit that we are in a cycle of behavior that is harming ourselves or others. The second part is admitting that we are currently lacking the life skills necessary to stop this cycle on our own.

In the practical version of this step, I use the term "self-destructive cycle" rather than "addiction" because I believe it's a more thorough and straightforward description of the problem. The term "addiction" has its place, but it is so often misunderstood that it tends to result in more confusion than it does clarity. If everyone could agree on a definition of "addiction," then I'd gladly incorporate it into this step. Until that time, I will refer to the problem we are seeking relief from as a self-destructive cycle, because that's essentially what it is. An added benefit of using this wording is that this step becomes applicable to any person who feels stuck instead of being limited to people that would traditionally be labeled "addicts."

Another piece to note about the practical version of the step is that it says we *currently* lacked the tools to control our behavior. The practical version of the steps are meant to be empowering, as opposed to the traditional version, which tells us that we are powerless and need to rely on God for help. By saying that we can be empowered, I'm not implying we can use drugs and alcohol moderately. I am still acknowledging the fact that there are some behaviors we will need to stop completely. What this step is saying is that we have the power and ability to make changes to our lifestyle and attitude that will help us remain free from our addictive behavior. Our healthy lifestyle will primarily be the result of *our* efforts rather than the intervention of a supreme being.

I've also done away with the term "unmanageability." All that's necessary for us to justify stopping a behavior is for it to be causing harm. Unmanageability may or may not be a part of an unhealthy cycle. It often is, but the term still tends to be too exclusive. There are plenty of addicts and alcoholics who have developed a tremendous talent for maintaining an impressive level of functioning despite their condition. Instead of trying to convince ourselves that we can't manage our own lives (a concept that is hard to define), we are asking ourselves a basic question: "is my addictive behavior causing harm to my life or the lives of others?"

By admitting that we are causing harm, we've given ourselves enough reason to change our ways. In addition, we rid ourselves of the denial that may be holding us back from facing the true nature of our condition. As I will discuss later in this book, being fully honest about our behavior is a crucial part of recovery. You can't get better from something you don't acknowledge. If you try to move ahead in the steps without first getting real about the state you're in, you may end up wasting a lot of time and effort.

No part of this step involves beating ourselves up or dwelling on our faults. It is meant to be a complete acceptance of what is. Nothing more, nothing less. We are not exaggerating our situation, nor are we minimizing it. In my experience, nothing good comes from distorting the reality of a situation. Scare tactics don't work and neither does denial. The only sane way to approach any problem is to approach it honestly and without reservation.

Working Step One

Working this step is fairly simple, but should be done thoughtfully. Take some time to explore this cycle you're stuck in. How did it start? Why was it so attractive at first? How have you tried to stop it? How, specifically, is it harming you and others? Have friends or loved ones expressed concerns about your cycle? It's also important to look at what occurs when you try and break out of the cycle. What emotions come up? What thoughts and excuses does your brain conjure up to try and convince you to stay in the cycle? Have you ever been able to stop, and if so, for how long? When you try to stop, are there replacement behaviors that you start engaging in instead (e.g. eating junk food, playing video games excessively, acting out sexually)?

Throughout this book, I will often suggest utilizing writing as a way of working the step. Sometimes it's necessary and sometimes it's optional. Doing some writing for step one is optional, but a great idea. One of the more powerful exercises I've seen people utilize is writing their story from childhood to the present moment, focusing on their use of addictive behaviors. Constructing a cohesive story about your journey to the doorstep of recovery can be a very effective way to gain some clarity and perspective on your current struggles. Oftentimes, when people look at their lives as a connected sequence of events, they're able to discover new patterns and gain some insight about how they got to their current state. This isn't necessarily the aim of this step, but it can help you understand why you got caught in your self-destructive cycle in the first place, which may also help you better accept the truth about your current condition.

Other options for working this step include having an in-depth conversation with your sponsor, therapist, or fellow recovering addicts/alcoholics. Take some time to explore how your cycle started. Was there an event that set things in motion? Did your self-destruction start quickly as a result of a traumatic life event or was it a gradual process that you didn't notice until it was well-established? What were the first consequences you noticed? How did you justify your behavior or make excuses? What did you consider your rock bottom, and was it an external event like jail or an internal event like depression or suicidal thinking? The more detailed you can get in this process, the better. If something feels too difficult to talk about, it's all the more reason to talk about it. Challenge yourself to move outside of your comfort zone.

You know you're done with this step when you can look at it without any reservations that it is true. You need to be pretty darn sure that your cycle is not something you can just snap out of through sheer willpower. It's important to be clear on this step or the following steps will be less effective. If there is any part of you that still thinks you can change your behavior without changing anything else in your life, it might be worth exploring this step further. If you're feeling stuck, chances are that a strong intention to stop your cycle is not enough on its own. That being said, if you aren't fully convinced that you need to change, it may be necessary to try it the old way for a while and experience some more failures before you're convinced. Some people need several attempts at pulling themselves up by their bootstraps before they realize they need assistance.

If you feel you've adequately explored your self-destructive cycle and come to terms with your current inability to stop it alone, then you're ready to begin step two. It's time to move from accepting your current inability to stop to believing that there is a way out.

I often divulged very private info to others - esp Mama. It was my way of getting close and I think it was encouraged... no boundaries at all... also the girls from highschool - we all put ourselves down as a way to relate or elevate the other or to get some positive attention of from the other person. I don't know if the binging started then although I do know that I made cookies or cake simply to eat or stuff myself on the batter of it. Of course everyone loved my baking, so it was encouraged.

I was/am aware of how much food I ate when I went off to school yet I lost weight during freshman year + gained more (the most I've ever weighed) the remaining years. This was when binging really set in...

Step Two

AA Version

Came to believe that a power greater than ourselves could restore us to sanity

Practical Version

Trusted that a healthy lifestyle was attainable through social support and consistent self-improvement

This step is a crucial part of preparing for the journey of recovery. It's about hope, optimism, and excitement. If you don't have any hope or excitement about this process, it's going to be much more difficult to engage in and commit to (step three). The AA version of this step focuses on the principle of faith. It asks for us to have faith that a power outside of ourselves will "restore us to sanity," that is, to correct our thinking. People have been basing their morals and "sanity" on supreme beings since the dawn of time, and it often doesn't turn out well. In the practical version of step two, we are acknowledging that we are the ones doing the work. Yes, we will get help from others. Yes, social support is important. We aren't doing this completely alone. That being said, *we* are still the primary driver of the process, not any other entity.

As a mental health professional, I think "sanity" is a poor word to use for this step. Granted, there are many aspects of addiction that seem insane, and some even technically meet the criteria for insanity. However, being restored to sanity implies that our goal is simply to not be insane. Don't get me wrong, not being insane is lovely, but we need more than that if we want to free ourselves from an addictive behavior that is dictating our lives. We don't just want sanity; we want mental and emotional health. Someone can be sane and still engage in behaviors that are damaging. It's possible to be fully aware of your addictive cycle, the harm it's causing, and still not be able to stop. Sanity is just the beginning.

A healthy lifestyle is a way of living in and relating to the world that minimizes the harm we cause ourselves and others. Ideally, a healthy lifestyle not only minimizes harm, but encourages regular, consistent growth. This is a mandatory part of recovery. We can't expect to remain free from addiction if we are still spending time with toxic people, avoiding processing our emotions, and engaging in unhealthy patterns of behavior. Living free from addiction requires a lifestyle change, full stop. The sooner this is realized, the sooner you can start getting better. Also, the more severe your addiction, the more your lifestyle will likely need to change. But fear not, this book will, at the very least, get you moving in the right direction.

While a healthy lifestyle is a necessity, it doesn't need to happen overnight. In fact, it usually can't and probably shouldn't. A healthy lifestyle is best attained (and maintained) through small, incremental changes. Trying to change too much too quickly often leads to feeling overwhelmed and can cause people to get discouraged, sometimes leading them to self-sabotage or experience burnout. The only exception is very early in recovery when you are still struggling to stay free of your addiction. At this stage, one of the best things you can do is perform a major restructuring of your social life by spending a lot of time with healthy people. This is yet another reason meetings have a lot to offer. Regardless of whether or not specific meetings support your God-free approach, you should try attending them. There will almost always be someone there who supports your non-belief. Tolerating the God talk early on is usually a necessary step while finding new meetings and developing new relationships. Connecting with people on the same path is paramount, and we'll get into this more in the chapters after the steps.

I realize that "self-improvement" is a broad term that means a lot of different things. The truth is, there is no aspect of self-improvement that won't also affect other areas of your life. For example, it's pretty near impossible to improve your physical health and not have it affect your mental health as well. Although all forms of self-improvement will benefit your overall wellness, some are a higher priority than others. In the case of this step, we want to start with the most fundamental areas of self-improvement such as self-care, personal responsibility, cultivating healthy relationships, and emotional intelligence. I don't expect you to know what all of these look like yet. They will be discussed and addressed in later steps. Also note that we are not yet actively taking specific actions towards self-improvement, we are simply acknowledging that doing so is necessary for achieving our goal of attaining a healthy lifestyle.

Working Step Two

One of my favorite exercises for this step is to vividly describe what a healthy lifestyle is. This can be done by writing a story, making a list, or creating a vision board. The goal is to cultivate a thorough vision of what you want your life to look like when you are free from the bonds of addiction. What will you be doing? What will your daily schedule look like? What will your goals be? What will you accomplish? What will your relationships look like? What kind of people will you spend your time with? What hobbies will you pursue? Where will you live and with whom? Your vision can be anything you want it to be. It's fine to aim high. In fact, it's preferred. This vision is being created with the knowledge that you may never achieve it perfectly. Part of the joy of recovering is the fact that there are always new ways you can continue to grow and improve. If you achieved perfection quickly, it might feel good for a bit, but it would eventually get pretty boring, don't you think?

Another key concept in this step is that of consistency. Working this step means developing an understanding of what consistency may look like for you as well as accepting the fact that it will be a crucial part of your recovery. The most successful sober individuals, religious or not, are the ones who make self-improvement a regular part of their daily lives. When people don't take the time and effort to regularly engage in self-improvement, they often start to repeat old patterns of behavior, which can eventually lead to relapse. You will obviously miss days here and there. I like the 80/20 rule, which states that succeeding at a commitment 80% of the time is perfectly acceptable. Let go of any perfectionism you might have and focus on being a little bit better than you were yesterday.

One of the most challenging parts of the original version of this step was determining when one had officially "come to believe." When I first worked step two, I obsessed over whether or not I believed strongly enough. It was often expressed by experienced members of the program that any sliver of doubt needed to be completely eradicated from my mind. For someone like myself who has a hard time with absolutes, this drove me a little nuts. Instead of telling you that you have to reach a state of complete, unquestioning belief, I'm asking you to trust this process based on evidence. At first, this evidence is the experience of other healthy individuals and the scientific research that supports the benefit of healthy habits. As you move along in the steps, your trust will be based more and more on the results that you're seeing in yourself.

Once you can say with a fair amount of confidence that you are capable of achieving a healthy lifestyle through regular self-improvement, you're ready to make a commitment to doing exactly that, which takes us to step three.

Step Three

AA Version

Made a decision to turn our will and our lives over to the care of God as we understood him

Practical Version

Committed to a lifestyle of recovery, focusing only on what we could control

The original version of this step is easily the most challenging for nonbelievers. We are expected to make a decision to turn our will (wants, desires, etc.) and life (behaviors) over to the care of a being that can't be seen, heard, or touched. It is a sticking point for many atheists and agnostics, and for good reason. Step two is doable for atheists and agnostics because they can just interpret a "power greater than ourselves" to mean lots of things that don't necessarily involve God. The third step, on the other hand, uses the word "God" explicitly, leaving little room for alternate interpretations. The practical version of this step keeps your life in your hands. Instead of turning anything over, you are empowering yourself to commit to a lifestyle of consistent self-improvement. Again, this doesn't mean you're doing this all without support from others, it just means you are the one driving the process and the rewards will primarily be a result of your efforts.

In this step, two major things are happening. First, you are not just deciding, but *committing*. A commitment is a big deal. It's more than nonchalantly telling yourself that you're going to give this recovery thing a go, it is making a pact with yourself and your support network to make this a non-negotiable priority in your life. This requires some thought and should not be glossed over. You are committing to fundamentally changing the way you live one gradual but meaningful step at a time. In order to do this, you need to feel done with your unhealthy patterns. You need to be able to picture your life without your toxic friends and toxic drama. If there is any significant part of you that is still holding on to your old way of living, you may need to approach this step with some diligence and remind yourself of why you wanted to recover in the first place. As with all things, this will ebb and flow. I don't expect you to never have a single thought of returning to your old ways, but it's important to make as strong a commitment as you are capable of.

The second significant action in this step is to shift our focus to the things we can control. I've worked with people in recovery for over a decade. Throughout my work, I have learned that the single most important shift that happens in a recovering person's mentality is the shift from blaming to taking responsibility. It is all too common to see desperate addicts come into 12-step meetings still focusing on the external situations that "made them" use drugs, whether it be their romantic partners, their bosses, their geographical location, or any other person or situation besides themselves. We are in recovery for one thing and one thing only: to change the way *we* behave and relate to the rest of the world. It's icing on the cake if things outside of our control fall into place, but expecting anything outside of our control to go a specific way is a recipe for frustration and resentment. Blaming others is characteristic of a victim mentality, which is disempowering. We're going for the opposite.

I am not denying the fact that many of us have been victims of the actions of others. There is a significant distinction between taking personal responsibility and taking blame. We are doing the former. Perhaps you were abused as a child (or adult). I would never suggest that a victim of abuse take the blame for what happened to them, but I would strongly suggest that he or she take responsibility for their life moving forward. Yes, you were wronged. Yes, it was horrible, but what now? Do we continue to waste our precious time and mental energy focusing on what should have happened, or do we process what happened, move through it, and heal? The more we focus on the things we can't control, the more we experience suffering. It's like wishing for the weather to change. The weather doesn't care what we want. It will do whatever the laws of physics dictate. We either choose to accept it or make ourselves miserable by dwelling over it. After we've shifted our focus to our own lives and the things we can control, we will be in a better position to identify our shortcomings and start taking actions to change them.

Working Step Three

For this step, I think it's best to have a sponsor, therapist, mentor, or trustworthy friend to go through it with. Making a commitment is more meaningful if you make it in the presence of other people. Accountability is a powerful tool in recovery. If somebody knows you're making this commitment, they can hold you to it and keep you honest. If you make the commitment alone in your bedroom with no witnesses, it will be easier to break.

Write a mission statement, an oath, or a contract in which you make a pledge to persistently lean toward a lifestyle of recovery. In this pledge, state your reasons for making this change, state when you will begin it, and state what your first actions will be. I'd suggest that your first action be to work through the rest of these steps, since that will create a foundation for you to then branch out and explore new avenues of self-improvement. Areas of self-improvement that aren't covered in the steps will be discussed after this chapter.

Find your partner for this step and read them the written commitment. After you've made the commitment, go someplace quiet and reflect for 15-20 minutes (or as long as you need to) on what just happened. Remember, this isn't like promising to do the laundry more often. You just committed to a new life. Soak it in and take some pride in it. After you take your time to reflect, go do something positive for yourself, even if it's just something mindless and fun.

Now that you've made this commitment, let's take our first concrete step in the direction of self-improvement: step four.

Step Four

AA Version

Made a searching and fearless moral inventory of ourselves

Practical Version

Made a comprehensive list of our resentments, fears, and harmful actions

Though I've changed the wording of step four, it is essentially saying the same thing in a simpler way. Morality is a thorny topic and means different things to different people, so I ditched that word in favor of plain language that simply describes what we're doing next. This step has the potential to be a powerful healing experience, but that is largely determined by the effort you put into it. People often get stuck on this step when looking at the sheer volume of writing that is required, not to mention the fact that the more time you've spent on this planet, the longer this step is likely to be. Don't let it overwhelm you. It is very doable and worth the time. As I previously mentioned, not all steps require some form of writing. This one does.

To begin, we look at resentments. The word "resent" comes from the French word "resentir," which literally means to re-feel. When you resent something that happened, you are playing it over and over in your mind and reliving the anger you experienced. This is a toxic cycle that can drive people back to unhealthy behaviors. The resentment can be something that resurfaces anywhere from once in a blue moon to every minute of the day. If it's a feeling of anger you're holding on to in any significant way, I would consider it a resentment and add it to your list.

Often, we develop resentments because we haven't fully processed the event we are stewing over. This step is going to give us an opportunity to process our resentments a little more thoroughly. This is done by looking at exactly why we were so hurt by what happened and also looking at whatever part we may have played in it. Remember that personal responsibility is a crucial part of recovery. We aren't taking the blame for what happened, but we are becoming willing to look at any unhealthy behavior that may have contributed to it.

We look at our fears next because they most likely have a significant impact on our lives. We humans are strongly motivated by fear. That's fine when our fear is over something like a mountain lion lunging towards us, but when our fears are exaggerated or irrational, they fuel irrational behavior. This step will attempt to unearth some of our core fears and self-defeating beliefs so we can challenge them and recognize how they may have held us back. It's not about eliminating fear, but about keeping our fears rational and in line with reality. Healthy fear is a good thing; irrational fear can be crippling.

Finally, we look at the people (or other sentient creatures) we have harmed. This stage is one of the best opportunities to identify your more destructive behavior patterns. Did you use people to get what you wanted? Did you lie? Did you manipulate? Were you physically violent? Sexually abusive? Emotionally abusive? All of the above? Again, this is going to be difficult to look at, so watch out for powerful feelings of guilt and shame. You'll need to remind yourself that this is not about feeling worse, it's about clearing out your conscience so you can feel free of the baggage that is weighing you down and contributing to your desire to escape. It's about feeling better and identifying what needs to change, but that means we have to do some difficult work.

Some clarification on the concept of shame: Shame is a powerful emotion that tends to cause more harm than it does good. Not to be confused with guilt, shame is a feeling that you are somehow bad or broken. Guilt is feeling like you did something wrong, shame is feeling like there is something wrong with *you*. While it may seem that shame would be motivating, it more often tends to keep people stuck. If you believe you're a broken human, you're less likely to feel hopeful about your future. It's much easier to believe you can fix a negative behavior than it is to believe you can fix something fundamental about who you are. If you find yourself sinking into a pit of shame, take a break, talk to a friend or sponsor, do something fun, or do something nice for someone else. Focus on your actions rather than your perceived value as a human being.

So, why are we even doing this? I'm glad you asked! We're doing this because we are beginning a journey of self-improvement, and you can't do that if you don't know what you need to improve. Step four is the beginning of a lifelong process (I know, there are lots of those) of learning about what makes you tick so you can make the necessary adjustments to your life. For example, let's say one of your primary sources of suffering is comparing yourself to other people and feeling inferior. You can't engage in the practices necessary to overcome that if you aren't even aware you're doing it. This step is a major stepping stone to uncovering the patterns in your behavior and thinking that may be keeping you from feeling confident and comfortable in your own skin.

It takes a long time and a lot of work to discover *all* of your unhealthy patterns. Most people never do. This is partly due to the fact that we all have several, but it's also due to the fact that we're often developing new ones without realizing it. Such is the way of life. All we can do is try to remain self-aware (we'll get more into this later when we talk about step ten) and nip our unhealthy patterns in the bud before they start causing serious harm. Ideally, we'll get to a place where our unhealthy patterns rear their ugly heads so infrequently that when they do arise, we notice quickly and take the appropriate actions to combat them.

During this step, it's common for people to uncover personality traits and behavior patterns that are difficult to face. For example, you may find out that you tend to discriminate against a certain group of people, or perhaps you have a need to feel superior. Maybe you've been a bully your whole life and never realized it until now. This can be difficult stuff to look at, so try to remember that this step is not about shame or beating yourself up. It's about looking as objectively as possible at how we live so that we can improve. Think of it as a scientific experiment. Science is about finding out the truth, not casting moral judgment.

This step is hard, there's no doubt about it, but it really gets a bad rap. It's often exciting and illuminating if you've never done anything like it before. Many people have never looked at their life anywhere near this closely, and it can be an intense experience. Some take to this very well, while others may get cold feet. If you find yourself really digging your heels in here, it's worth exploring why. Be honest about it with your support system. Talk about what you're afraid or skeptical of. Does the task feel insurmountable? Do you worry that you'll do it and nothing will get better? Do you think it's a waste of time? Do you feel like it's nothing more than "dwelling" that will ultimately make you feel worse about yourself? These are all normal and understandable concerns to have. The neat thing about being concerned is that it doesn't have to stop you. If you're concerned, that's ok. Do it anyway. You'll never know if your concerns are justified until you try. In the end, if it turns out this was a waste of time, what have you really lost other than a few hours and some pen ink? In my experience, however, it's damn near impossible to do such a thorough examination of your life without it changing you in some positive way.

If you have been or currently are in therapy, it's possible this step will come a little bit easier to you. There's nothing wrong with that, but don't assume that your therapy has uncovered everything and that you can skip this step. Even us therapists have blind spots. Writing a comprehensive list is different than talking to someone in an office for 50 minutes at a time. It's not better or worse, just different. It gives you the opportunity to look at your life through a different lens, which may provide you with insights you would have otherwise missed. Therapy isn't a replacement for this step, nor is this step a replacement for therapy. The two are unique and can coexist quite perfectly. In fact, it would be an excellent idea to go over some or all of this list with your therapist.

Working Step Four

Without question, the process of working step four has had the most debate amongst 12-step gurus. Some say the list should have four columns, others say three, and some have developed their own versions with a combination of columns and checkboxes. It's my goal to create a version that is thorough but simple, and I believe I've done so. If you or your sponsor feel there is any extra information to add, feel free to add additional columns for that.

It's my personal experience that doing this work is equally effective whether you do it by hand or digitally on a computer. Some people claim that doing this step with pen and paper has a certain magic to it. Do whatever works best for you. The point is to do it mindfully and as thoroughly as possible. If writing this step by hand helps you feel more connected to the process, then do it. If you dislike writing by hand (like I do), feel free to do it on a spreadsheet program or word processor. I don't believe it makes that much of a difference as long as you aren't rushing through it to get it over with.

We'll begin with the resentment list because resentments are often a significant portion of our emotional baggage. The list will contain four columns: who the person, group, or institution is, what they did, how it hurt you, and what your part is (if anything). You may have heard that we have a part in all our resentments. I think this is usually true, but there are exceptions. If you honestly look at your part and believe you couldn't have done anything different, instead use the fourth column to look at what is causing you to hold on to the resentment. Is it unwillingness to forgive? Is it a desire for revenge? Is there some payoff to identifying as a victim?

Regardless of what was done to you, today you have the power to respond to your feelings about it even if you couldn't respond differently to the event itself.

It's worthwhile to note that there is significant research to support the reality that early childhood trauma, neglect, and abuse can significantly increase one's risk of addiction and other destructive behaviors[5]. Knowing this, I implore you to spend extra time looking at your early childhood. If you question whether or not something belongs on this list, write it down anyway. Worst case scenario, you decide it's not relevant and pay it no mind. If this process drums up some traumatic wounds that you have trouble coping with, please find a professional to talk to about it. Trauma and unresolved grief and loss are toxic and often require the assistance of a well-trained therapist or counselor.

For all of the lists in this step, we fill them out by columns first, meaning we write all our names from top to bottom, then move on to the 2nd column for each entry, etc. When you read them, you'll read them across. Writing them across, however, makes it too challenging for most. You'll likely find that you have to get into a "zone" when doing each particular column. Shifting your focus for each entry gets tiring and can cause people to burn out quickly. Start with all the entries in column one, then move on to column two, and so on.

For the first column of this list, we are listing all the people, groups, or institutions that we currently resent. It's going to take some time to come up with this list, and you'll likely remember more names as you progress. Do your best to list as many people as possible, even if the resentment feels nearly nonexistent. If you're having trouble remembering people, it may be helpful to develop a systematic way of combing through your history. For example, you may want to go by grade when doing your school-age resentments. Think about who you resented in first grade, second grade, third grade, and so forth. When you're looking at your adult years, you can go by jobs, areas in which you lived, or any theme that helps you ensure you're looking at everything.

For the second column, we are listing the specific action that caused us resentment. As with all lists in this step, we want to stick to facts. This isn't a place to unload your anger and write about what a horrible human being this person is. While that may feel good, it makes it more difficult to look at your part (column four). By sticking to facts, it's easier to see where you might have misinterpreted or made assumptions about the other person's action. For example, instead of writing, "Cindy tried to steal my boyfriend," you would write, "Cindy texted my boyfriend in a flirtatious manner." Unless you have direct evidence to support the belief that Cindy was literally trying to take your boyfriend away from you, the first entry contains assumptions that are possibly incorrect.

In the third column, we are looking at emotional and practical impacts that this behavior had or is having on you. Perhaps this behavior caused you to feel unsafe or unimportant. Maybe you felt helpless or frightened. Maybe it costed you money, time, or impacted your relationships. Whatever the affect is, write it here. For this column, all that matters is your experience. It doesn't matter at this point whether or not your feelings were based on distorted thinking or not. You're only focusing on your subjective experience. We'll analyze it a bit more in step six.

The fourth column is where a lot of the magic happens in this list. It's not overstating it to say that shifting your focus from the actions of others to your own actions is a change that will revolutionize your life. It doesn't matter if a situation occurred in which the other person was 99% wrong and you were only 1% wrong. When you learn to let go of how the other person was wrong and instead look at where you acted unskillfully, you will experience a new level of personal growth and freedom from resentment. Blaming others for your problems may provide some relief in the moment, but in the long term it cements in a belief that you are at the mercy of others. You have more power over your life and circumstances than you think, and you won't discover that power until you stop believing it belongs to other people.

I'll illustrate this concept with an extreme example. Let's say you were driving and honked briefly at someone in front of you for going too slowly. That person then gets out of his or her car, walks over to you, asks you to roll down the window, and punches you in the nose. It's certainly safe to say that you shouldn't have been punched. I'd be perfectly fine to admit that this person was 99% in the wrong. That being said, what good is it going to do you to carry around anger at this person? You can stew over the fact that he or she acted completely irrationally, but how does that help you? Wouldn't it be more helpful to look at what you did in this situation and grow from it? Were you maybe being impatient and acting mildly aggressively? That's something you can do something about; the other person's behavior isn't. I'll repeat for emphasis that this is *not* victim-blaming. You did not deserve to get punched. That was wrong and that person committed a crime and ideally will be held accountable for it. What you're doing is looking at any sliver of responsibility that you can find and using the information to grow into a better human being.

Looking at your part does not absolve the other person, it

just gives you permission to let go of resentment and find an opportunity to become a better person. It can even allow you to muster some empathy for the offending person. Maybe they were having a terrible day after getting fired and your impatience was the straw that broke the camel's back. Is that an excuse? No. Is it something you can relate to as a human being? Possibly, and that empathy will allow you to more completely let go of your resentment.

Here is an example of a couple rows from a resentment list:

Who	What they did	Impact	My part
My neighbor Joe	Ignored me last month when I said "hi" to him.	Felt embarrassed, hurt, angry. Felt uncomfortable in my own neighborhood	I once criticized him in a rude manner when he was playing loud music at night.
My mother	Used to call me "stupid" when I would make a mistake.	I felt ashamed and unsure of myself. Lost confidence in myself. Thought my mom didn't love me.	I'm lacking empathy for her. She had an abusive childhood and probably thought what she was doing was OK.

Notice that the entry about "my mother" takes a different approach in the fourth column. It's safe to say that being verbally abused by a parent is not something you had a part in as a child. Sure, you may have colored on the walls or broken something, but you were too young to know any better. That being said, you now have a part in holding on to that resentment. Use the fourth column to explore why you're holding on to that resentment and what may be keeping you from letting it go.

Forgiveness and compassion are powerful tools for dealing with resentments. A popular suggestion in 12-step meetings is to pray for the person you resent. The reason this often works is because it forces you to practice compassion. It's pretty near impossible to feel compassion and resentment for someone at the same time. Those who hurt others are usually doing so because of some pain they themselves are living with. If you can find it within yourself to seek an understanding of their pain-driven behavior, it can be a tremendous relief. Remember that forgiveness is not something you're doing for the other person; you're doing it to free yourself from the suffering that comes from harboring those toxic thoughts about them.

Once you feel satisfied that you've completed the resentment list to the best of your ability, it's time to tackle the fear list. This list should include everything from embedded core beliefs to mild anxieties. If you're terrified of being abandoned, put that on the list. If you're slightly worried about getting demoted at work, put that on the list, too. It's all important. All of these fears add up and can take a toll on your mental health if they aren't addressed. Unfortunately, many people today think that acknowledging fears is weakness and that avoiding them is strength. The opposite is true. It takes a lot more effort to face a fear than it does to pretend it doesn't exist.

The fear list consists of three columns: what you fear, a core belief that drives this fear, and a reality-based replacement belief. I know those last two columns may sound a bit complicated, but don't worry, I'll be walking you through them. This list is similar to a common cognitive-behavioral[6] exercise known as an automatic thought record. Cognitive-behavioral therapy is one of the most well-studied forms of psychotherapy and has been shown to improve a wide range of conditions including anxiety, depression, and addictive behaviors[7].

The first column is pretty self-explanatory. Write out what you are afraid of in as much detail as you feel is necessary. You can either keep it simple (e.g. "Abandonment,") or you can be more descriptive (e.g. "Worried people will hate me if I disappoint them.") Generally speaking, more detail can help you with the next column when you have to break the fear apart and look for the distorted belief that is fueling it.

The second column is where things get really interesting. You may have never heard of a "core belief" before. Core beliefs are things we believe (either consciously or subconsciously) about ourselves, the world, or the people in it. When we are experiencing an irrational fear, it is often due to an underlying core belief that is distorted, meaning it's exaggerated or unrealistic. I've listed some common distorted core beliefs and fears that may stem from them. Feel free to use some of these, but know that this list is not exhaustive.

Distorted core belief	Fears that result
"The world is unsafe"	- Being the victim of a crime - Being betrayed - Suddenly losing a loved one - Getting into an accident
"I am unlovable"	- Being abandoned - Being alone - Being hated - Being judged
"I'm incompetent"	- Failing - Harming others unintentionally - Saying something stupid or embarrassing - Not being able to learn a new skill
"Nothing works out for me"	- Ruining relationships - Messing up a plan - Failing when trying something new - Being a bad parent to your future children

This list should hopefully give you a starting point and a better understanding of what the second column is looking for. If you have a fear of getting fired, for example, it could very well be coming from a belief that you are not good enough, incompetent, unlikeable, etc. This step is going to take some time, especially if you've never done this kind of work before. With practice, you'll get better at it. You'll also start to notice that many of your fears stem from a common core belief. Once you get a good idea of what your most prominent negative core beliefs are, you'll have good material with which to begin the third column.

The third column is where we write a replacement belief to tell ourselves in place of our distorted belief. We want this belief to be reality-based, which means it isn't overly positive, nor is it excessively negative. When it comes to writing a replacement fear, do your best to stick to simple statements that are as factual-sounding as possible but also empowering. You may not believe these alternative beliefs yet, but that doesn't matter. Incorporating them into our lives comes in a later step. Look at the available evidence to support your new beliefs.

To give an example, below are some negative core beliefs along with some more reality-based beliefs to counter them.

Distorted core belief	Alternate realistic belief
The world is unsafe.	There's always a small risk of something bad happening. I can minimize the chances by being safe.
I am unlovable.	I have lovable traits that I can learn to nurture.
I am incompetent.	I am capable of learning just like everyone else. There are several things I'm knowledgeable about.
Nothing works out for me.	Some things work out for me and some don't. I can choose to focus more on the things that do work.

I'm beyond fixing.	It's never too late to make myself better.

Again, feel free to use these if they fit for you. If not, take the time to develop ones that do. Some of the alternate realistic beliefs will no doubt sound corny and fake to you at first. That's completely normal. Just keep listing these out until you have one for each of your negative core beliefs. Once you finish this column, you're done with the fear list.

The final list is one of the toughest. We are going to make a list of people we've hurt. Remember that we aren't just focusing on people who were innocent victims—we're focusing on *anyone* we've hurt, even if they hurt us. It doesn't matter if the person who was hurt by us "deserved it" or hurt us first. We are only focusing on our actions alone. We have no control over the actions of others. By focusing on ourselves, we are better able to see what our patterns are and what we need to work on.

This is the last part of step four. It consists of three columns: who you hurt, how you hurt them, and how they may have been impacted by your action. The first column lists the person (or company, institution, etc.) that you hurt by name alone. The second column is the specific harmful action that you engaged in. The third column is how this action may have had an impact on the victim. If this still sounds a little complicated, I promise it will make sense soon. By the end of this section, you'll have a very clear idea of how to do this.

The first column is just a name. It can be the name of an institution, company, group, or individual. For example, if you stole from Blockbuster Video as a teenager, you just write "Blockbuster Video." However, if you harmed any specific people who were working for an institution, you would list them instead of the institution. If you yelled and cursed at a Blockbuster employee, for example, you would put that employee's name (or a description if you can't remember his or her name) instead. You didn't harm Blockbuster by yelling at an employee; you harmed that employee.

The second column is what you did. This is where you write down the specific action that you engaged in. It is essential that you stick to facts and *do not minimize*. We are doing this to take full responsibility for our past misdeeds, not to save face or make excuses. An entry may say something to the effect of, "I borrowed money from Joe and promised I would pay him back, but never did." It's straight, simple, and to the point. You're not explaining why Joe deserved it or how he has tons of money and it isn't a big deal. You're saying what you did. No more and no less.

The third column is where we practice empathy for the victim. Oftentimes, we engage in behaviors that harm people and give no thought to how it may harm them. Even if we think we know, we don't always give it the level of thought that is warranted. For example, after not paying Joe back, he may have felt used, betrayed, insulted, or angry. It's possible it may have even put financial strain on him. It's also important to stay away from the phrase "I made him angry/sad/scared." Stating that you "made" someone feel a certain way implies we have more power over them than we do. They may feel a certain way about our actions, but we didn't directly control their feelings.

You can also make some basic assumptions in this column. For example, it's possible Joe was financially stressed because of this, but it's also possible he wasn't. Either way, it can be useful to look at the risks that were taken when engaging in these harmful or potentially harmful actions. If you drove recklessly, for example, you may have never crashed, but it's important to put it on your list and acknowledge that you put the safety of others at risk. Stay reasonable, though. You don't want to go into fantasy land and make up far-fetched scenarios, but don't ignore the obvious risks either.

For some reason I have yet to fully understand, the original instructions for doing the last part of the fourth step focus solely on sexual misconduct[8]. Clearly, addicts (and non-addicts, for that matter) can cause some serious harm in the sexual arena; we are more than capable. That being said, there aren't many reasons (other than stigma and religious beliefs) that I can see to make sexual behavior its own special category. Just don't neglect to think about it when compiling your list of harms. Were there people you harassed? People you sexually assaulted or took advantage of? Did you break any laws? Did you manipulate people's emotions for sex? Did you abuse pornography at the expense of your intimacy with your significant other? Did you pay for sex and possibly contribute to sexual trafficking? All of these are questions to consider when writing this list.

At this point, you've done a lot of writing. The good news is, you're done writing for a while and will not have to do this much writing anywhere else in the steps. If you love writing and find it helpful, you're welcome to do this as often as you'd like. The rest of you can put your pens down. Take a look at these lists you've put together and bask for a while in the accomplishment. You've thoroughly explored some of the most complicated and potentially messy areas of your life, and you did it bravely. The vast majority of people in the world will never do this type of deep digging into their psyche. Be proud of what you've accomplished so far—be proud enough to want to share it, because that's next.

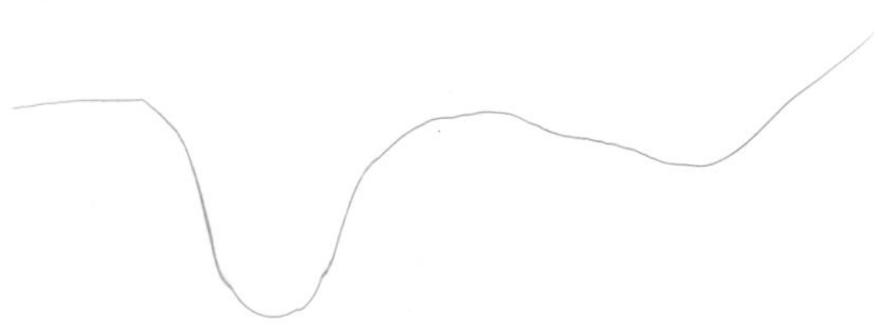

Step Five

AA Version

Admitted to God, to ourselves, and to another human being the exact nature of our wrongs

Practical Version

Shared our lists with a trustworthy person

Step four is a good amount of difficult writing. Now get ready for some difficult talking. More likely than not, it's going to feel uncomfortable to share such intimate details with someone else. Ideally, you want to pick someone who is experienced in recovery, such as a sponsor or a therapist. It should also be someone with whom you've spent some time and gotten comfortable. It's probably best to avoid picking a family member or a very close friend, and instead pick someone who is more of a guide or mentor in your life. Having trust in the person you pick is also crucial for obvious reasons.

Step five serves two very important purposes. First, it gives you an opportunity to clear your conscience by opening up about things that you've likely kept secret for a long time. Not only that, but the person you read these lists to will likely be one of the first people in your life to ever get a full picture of your "darker" side. It's possible you've told a few people different bits of your story, but having someone who knows everything can feel very liberating. You are no longer alone with the knowledge of your resentments, fears, and harms.

The second purpose of step five is to give yourself the opportunity to receive some objective feedback about your behavior patterns. We all have blind spots when it comes to looking at our own behavior. No matter how closely we scrutinize our lists, we will probably miss a few things. Giving all of this information to a third party can afford us a chance to hear someone else's take on our history. We have to let our defenses down as much as possible and be willing to hear feedback that hurts. If any of these steps were easy, they wouldn't be helping you grow.

If you can't seem to find anyone to do this step with, do not give up. There is truly no substitute to doing this with a caring and attentive partner. Go to different meetings or even check out a different fellowship if you need to. You may want to attend some online meetings and ask people you meet there. Face-to-face is always preferred, but some people live in areas where 12-step members are difficult to come by. Most of the bigger fellowships these days have regular phone or online meetings that you can find with a quick internet search. Don't be shy about asking someone during the meeting if they'd be willing to listen to your fifth step. Just make sure it's someone who seems to have some experience and isn't brand new to the program.

This may be an unpopular opinion, but I firmly believe that there are some people in the program (even long-timers) who have no business leading people through any of the steps, let alone one as personal as this. It doesn't necessarily mean there's anything wrong with their recovery, it just means they aren't the teaching type. Most sponsors probably have the basic skillset to give you some useful feedback, but if your partner seems to be giving you feedback that just doesn't make sense or feels way off the mark, don't discount the possibility that you should try doing this step again with someone else.

Working Step Five

Working this step will be a slightly different process depending on the person with whom you're sharing it. A sponsor with lots of experience may have a particular way he or she likes to do the fifth step. That's totally fine. What's important is that you're given the opportunity to read it as is and that the listener is willing to provide feedback based on his or her observations. Remember that the person listening to this step is a human being who doesn't have all the answers and has a unique point of view. If you do this step with 50 people, you'll get 50 different sets of feedback. Don't take your partner's feedback as gospel, but do consider it carefully and without defensiveness. If something your step five partner says truly feels inaccurate, that's OK. Set it aside and move on.

Some people like to do this step in a public place like a coffee shop or a park. I suppose that's acceptable if you truly feel comfortable in that setting. However, if you are at all on edge or anxious during this process, you're going to have a much more difficult time getting through it openly and honestly. You may censor yourself or hold back for fear of being overheard by people around you. I highly suggest doing this step in somebody's home, either yours or your partner's. If you can't, or if you both live with other people, it's worth it to look at alternate places to do this step where you won't be interrupted.

This step can potentially take anywhere from an hour to most of the day. It depends on how long your lists are. Make sure you're prepared. Get a full night's sleep the night before and make sure you stay nourished. If you try and get this step done in one fell swoop and don't take breaks to eat and rest, your ability to stay present through it will suffer. This process is about being thorough, not fast. If you need to split this up over two or more days, then go ahead and do that. It's better than rushing through it and missing out on the full experience.

Read this step one row at a time. You wrote this step one column at a time, but reading it that way doesn't make much sense. After you read each row, give your partner an opportunity to provide you with some feedback. If he or she has some, make note of it. If not, move on to the next row. Resist the urge to make excuses when it comes to reading these lists. Remember, you are just sticking to the facts and reading it exactly as it has been written unless your partner asks for clarification. You may feel very vulnerable during this process, but try to avoid explaining yourself or justifying your behavior. If you are feeling overcome with shame or embarrassment, mention it to your partner and ask to take a break.

After you finish reading these lists off, take some time to be by yourself and let yourself wind down and de-stress. It's highly likely that you'll be in the midst of a flurry of mixed emotions at this point. This is an excellent opportunity to relax and allow your mind to sort through all the emotions that have just been stirred up. I recommend going someplace quiet such as your bedroom and doing nothing. Don't read, don't watch TV, and don't listen to music. Just spend a good 30-60 minutes being alone with yourself. If you need more time, great, but don't spend less than 30 minutes doing this. If you have any major insights that you simply must take note of, then go ahead and write them down, but it would be ideal to save it until after you finish sitting quietly.

Some people like to throw away or burn their fourth step

after reading it. You're free to do that, but keep it around for a while longer so you can use it to help with step six. It will come in handy when you're compiling your list of unhealthy character traits. Once you're done with that, I'm all for ceremoniously disposing of your fourth step however you may choose. It can be a very cleansing experience, especially if you have someone (like your fifth step partner) there to partake in the ritual with you. If you'd prefer to keep it, that's fine, too. It can be a pretty eye-opening experience to look back on it years later after you've made significant growth in your life.

Step Six

AA Version
Were entirely ready to have God remove all these defects of character
Practical Version
Made a list of our unhealthy character traits

If you're the kind of person to pick up a book like this, you're also probably the kind of person to bristle when reading the original version of this step. It's not at all far-fetched to conclude that this step is telling us we have certain aspects of ourselves that are defective and can only be remedied by asking a supernatural being to take them away. As a psychotherapist, I obviously disagree with this sentiment. I would be lying and doing a disservice to my clients if I told them, "Well, you have a slew of character defects that neither of us can do anything about. You should probably ask the creator of the universe to take them away."

The practical version of this step takes a very different approach. We currently possess character traits that have entered unhealthy territory. Referring to them as "unhealthy" implies that we can make them healthy again. The term "defective" is far more pessimistic and suggests there is some fundamental flaw that we possess. We are not defective; we have developed thought and behavior patterns that once served a purpose, but have become dysfunctional. Most of these so-called character defects are actually character assets that have been taken to an extreme in response to life events. For example, if we're selfish, it could very well be that we didn't get our needs met in childhood and therefore had to hyper-focus on ourselves (a common precursor to narcissism). It was a coping strategy at the time, but now our circumstances have changed and this tendency causes more harm than good.

As is most of the work in these steps, this part of the process is simple but not easy. We are trying to shape our character traits over a period of time. Shaping is a process that requires consistency and discipline. Sometimes the changes will occur fairly quickly, but more often than not, they will occur at a slower pace than we would like. The more work you put into shaping these new character traits, the faster they are likely to develop. At first, we will be looking to change the most destructive character traits that we possess. As we progress, our effort will be geared more towards fine-tuning aspects of our self that keep us from being our healthiest, which, you guessed it, is a lifelong process.

Your fourth step will come in handy here. It will allow you to get a bird's-eye view of your behavior and try to identify commonalities between all of your resentments, fears, and harms. I'll provide some samples in the section about working this step to help you get started. However, the end goal here is not just to end up with a list of our unhealthy character traits, but to end up with a list of *healthy* character traits that we want to practice cultivating by practicing healthy behaviors. For example, if you tend to be selfish, the way you become less of a selfish person is to do more for others. At first the new behaviors will feel forced an unnatural, but they will eventually become habits, and will therefore result in the development of new character traits.

Working Step Six

People often worked the original version of this step by simply uttering a prayer stating that they were "entirely ready" to have these character traits removed. While I do think it will be helpful to be motivated, the idea of needing to be entirely ready in order to begin a process of change is a misleading one. All you need is to be ready enough to take the first action. So, if you're ready enough, take a look at your fourth step and make sure you have a sheet of paper (or word processor) available to make a list of your unhealthy character traits.

Start by looking at the "my part" column of your resentment list. What do you see there? What character traits pop out at you as you read down the column? Remember that we previously read this list one row at a time for step five, so reading just the fourth column from top to bottom should be a new experience for you. It will give you an opportunity to more easily see recurring patterns in your behavior. As you read each entry of the fourth column, write one or two words next to it briefly describing the unhealthy character trait (or traits) involved. For example, if your fourth column states something like, "I took advantage of his trust" you may write something like, "manipulation" or "dishonesty" next to it.

Next, look at your fears list. More specifically, look at your negative core beliefs. For example, if you have a negative core belief that you don't deserve to be happy, what unhealthy character traits might be fueling that belief? Is it insecurity? Self-hate? Self-judgement? All of the above? Whatever they are, write them down next to the appropriate row on your fears list. There will probably be quite a bit of repetition. That's actually a good thing. It's what enables us to identify the patterns we're looking for.

Finally, look at your harms list. Look at each harm and consider what negative character trait enabled you to cause that harm. If you stole from someone, what negative character traits do you think allowed you to do that? Perhaps you were entitled and felt you deserved their possession more than they did. Perhaps you judged them for having more than you. Perhaps you wanted more than you already had, and were therefore operating out of greed. Maybe you were impatient and wanted to get something the easy way instead of earning it. Many unhealthy character traits can apply to one behavior, so jot down as many as you can that you believe apply to you.

When you've completed your list, look for any character defects that can be put under the same umbrella. For example, if you listed "don't do much for others" and "only think about myself" as two separate character traits, you can probably put both of them under the umbrella of selfishness. We want to keep this list as concise as possible because it's going to determine what we do in step seven. If we have too many highly specific unhealthy character traits, it's going to be more complicated later on when we try to come up with behaviors to counter each unhealthy character trait.

I've created a fairly comprehensive list of unhealthy character traits below. However, I don't suggest using this list as your only source. Take the time and effort to think for yourself and put your unhealthy character traits into your own words. Go ahead and use this list to guide you, but if you can think of ones that aren't on this list, please add them yourself. You'll see that these are mostly single-word descriptions. This is because we want to look at core character traits. If your explanation of an unhealthy character trait is long and complicated, it's probably a small part of a larger pattern.

Examples of unhealthy character traits		
Selfishness	Ignorance	Judgment
Avoidance	Dishonesty	Aggression
Jealousy/Envy	Entitlement	Apathy
Manipulation	Arrogance	Insecurity
Overthinking	Self-hate	Greed
Vindictiveness	Impatience	Vanity
Self-pity	Blame	Stubbornness
Indecisiveness	Paranoia	Cynicism

Don't worry about having a perfect list. You'll probably add on to it later. Also, keep in mind throughout this process that any of these 12 steps can be revisited at any time. In fact, the maintenance portion of the program (steps 10, 11, and 12) is essentially a regular revisiting of all previous steps in some form or another. Let go of the desire to do everything perfectly the first time around.

As soon as you feel confident that you have a decently thorough list of your unhealthy character traits, you'll be ready to move on to step seven.

Step Seven

AA Version
Humbly asked him to remove our shortcomings

Practical Version
Began cultivating healthy character traits through consistent positive behavior

Congratulations! You get to finally start *practicing* this stuff in your daily life. Up until now, we've been making lots of lists and doing lots of analysis. The reason I've approached the steps this way is to ensure that we have a very solid foundation before we start implementing new behaviors. It's important that we have a full picture of our starting point before we begin taking practical actions. Don't get me wrong, everything you've done so far has been hard work and may have already started to elicit a change, but this is the point where you actively bring what you've learned into the world and into your interactions with yourself and others.

If someone tells you not to think about a pink elephant, you're going to think about a pink elephant. You're probably thinking of a pink elephant right now thanks to me. We aren't very good at *not* thinking about things. It's just not something our brains do. We are far better at focusing on something specific. If I don't want you to think about a pink elephant, I'll have better success by telling you to think about a blue giraffe. Knowing that, isn't it probably best for us to focus on how we should behave rather than how we shouldn't?

The original step mentions what we should be rid of, but doesn't tell us what to replace it with. In the practical version of this step, we are focusing only on what we are adding to our lives. We are cultivating healthy character traits (I like to call them "goal traits") through consistent, positive behavior. The step says nothing about what we are getting rid of because that just doesn't work. If you want to stop being selfish, practice generosity. If you want to stop being manipulative, practice direct and assertive communication. If you want to stop being entitled, practice gratitude. Your unhealthy character traits will naturally diminish when you start practicing behaviors that nourish your goal traits. If you focus daily on being a generous person, it's going to start feeling really strange and uncomfortable when you act selfishly, because it's not what you're used to anymore. Your regular behavior of generosity has made you a more generous person and less of a selfish one. You've elicited a change in yourself.

Notice I used the word, "cultivate." We aren't flipping a switch and suddenly becoming selfless, nor are we doing a week-long personality makeover boot camp. This is a process that is going to last us the rest of our days. We are cultivating it like one would cultivate a garden. Think of your goal traits as the plants and your positive behaviors as the soil and water. We are watering our goal traits one behavior at a time over a lifetime. This process will have its ups and downs. There will be days where practicing your healthy behaviors is a challenge and others where it comes easily. That is completely normal and nothing to beat yourself up over as long as you commit to practicing them again the following day.

The other key word in this step is "consistency." This step only works if you are consistent in your practice. It's not going to do you a lot of good to practice honesty for one week and then stop. No, you won't lose all your progress if you skip a day, but if you stop practicing these behaviors altogether, it's quite possible that you will revert back to less desirable behaviors that are more deeply embedded in your psyche. There are some goal traits that will be very hard to develop and may never get to where you want them to be, but you'd be surprised how much we can change with dedication and regular practice.

You may wonder what the end goal of all of this work is. Are we changing these unhealthy character traits because we care what other people think of us? Are we doing it because it's the "right" thing to do? Are we doing it to be more successful in certain areas of our lives? Improving your character can certainly help with all of these things, but the ultimate goal, as far as this book is concerned, is minimizing the stress and drama in your life and improving the quality of your relationships. Toxic behavior attracts toxic people that bring more toxic behavior to your life. If you want to surround yourself with positive, healthy people (step twelve), you need to be a positive, healthy person (most of the time, anyway). If you continue engaging regularly in your harmful, unhealthy behaviors, healthy people will avoid letting you into their lives, because that's what healthy people do. Be the kind of person you want to attract into your life.

Working Step Seven

Now, take a look at that cringe-inducing list of unhealthy character traits. Before we get started, I want you to take a second to accept them all as part of who you currently are. Try to avoid looking at them with judgment. All of these traits served a purpose at some point in your life. Maybe being aggressive and violent was a necessary defense mechanism in the neighborhood in which you grew up. Maybe your apathy exists because you struggled to get your needs met as a child and had no room to develop empathy for others. Maybe you tend to avoid dealing with uncomfortable situations because you never had role models that taught you healthy coping skills. Whatever the cause, try to have some compassion for yourself. These are survival mechanisms that have become old and outdated. If you want to replace them with new ones, you need to first let go of any shame or guilt you have around possessing them.

In this step, we will not be focusing on getting rid of unhealthy character traits, but on building goal traits that counter our unhealthy ones. This may sound like mincing words, but there is a difference. Moving towards something positive is a much different experience than trying to move away from something negative. We are growing and improving ourselves, not amputating parts of our personality. In some situations, we will need to focus on abstaining from behaviors, but most of the time we'll be focusing on practicing new behaviors.

Looking at your list of unhealthy character traits, think of a goal trait to counter each one and write it next to the original trait. For example, if you have "entitlement" as one of your unhealthy character traits, you would write something like "gratefulness" next to it. It may take some thinking to come up with a goal trait for every unhealthy trait, so don't feel shy about asking a sponsor or counselor for help. Keep this list somewhere where you can regularly revisit it.

It's unreasonable to expect yourself to start working towards all of your goal traits at once. You're probably going to have more success if you pick one or two to focus on at first. Over time, you'll get familiar enough with your goal traits that you'll be able to keep them all in mind throughout your daily life. For now, however, let's determine which ones to start with. One of the first I always recommend working on is honesty. If honesty isn't on your list, it should be. I have yet to meet an addict or alcoholic that doesn't engage in some form of lying or secrecy, and few things are as toxic to us and our relationships as dishonesty is. As a bonus, practicing honesty also helps us learn how to speak assertively (something I'll get into more later) and pushes us to become more aware of our emotions so we can communicate them and respond to them truthfully.

If you feel there are more important character traits that you want to build first, go for it. Writing a hierarchy of least to most important character traits can help you determine which ones you want to work on first. I find it to be more rewarding to work on the ones you seem to lack the most, but if you feel that's too difficult or you're not making progress, it's fine to focus on something easier for a while. You can always come back to the trait that you're having trouble with. Just be sure not to avoid the difficult stuff out of fear. The only way you can fail at this step is to not try new behaviors.

Once you've decided on the goal trait or traits you want to start developing, write them out on a post-it or piece of paper and put that somewhere where you'll see it regularly like on your bedroom door or taped to your wallet. The point is to remind yourself often that this is a plant you need to be watering. If you look in the bathroom mirror every morning and see the words "honesty" and "gratefulness," you are going to be more likely to remember to practice developing those traits that day.

Next, it's time to consider the actual behaviors that will be used to move you closer to possessing your goal trait. Make a list if it helps (and you aren't sick of making lists by now). If the behavior is something you can do at any time, make an effort to practice one or two of them a day, even if the behaviors seem small and irrelevant (e.g. holding a door open for someone). If it helps to plan the behaviors ahead of time, you can do that, but you can't always plan for opportunities to practice your positive behaviors. Sometimes, a situation will present itself and you'll have to act accordingly without much time to plan. For example, your spouse may notice you're quiet and ask you how you're feeling, which provides you with an opportunity to practice honesty. You'll have to decide in a matter of moments whether or not you want to respond with a typical, "I'm fine" or with something more honest like, "I feel like crap because I got reprimanded at work." This is something that you'll get better at over time and is part of the reason we remind ourselves of our goal trait often.

The next section goes into a little more detail regarding specific goal traits and how we can start developing them. As usual, this list doesn't include every positive character trait in the world, so if you can think of others that apply to you, don't leave them off your list.

Honesty

Honesty is easily one of the most important character traits to possess if you want to live a happy, relatively drama-free life. Nothing seems to weigh so heavily on our conscience as secrets and lies. Being honest doesn't just mean telling the truth, it also means acting with integrity—that is, living according to your values. It means showing up to work on time even if nobody will notice you're late. It means bringing up relationship concerns with your significant other instead of sweeping them under the rug. It means doing the right thing even when nobody is looking.

There are ample opportunities to practice honesty in life. To start very simply, tell the truth when speaking. If you feel the desire to speak words that are exaggerated or untrue, instead speak from a place of truth. It will be uncomfortable at first, especially if lying is one of your primary methods of avoiding conflict. However, you will soon get used to it and it will become a way of life. You will feel lighter, more free, and more confident in yourself. It's a glorious feeling to walk around without the burden of having to maintain lies. Many addicts get so far into their addiction that they end up living double lives. That simply has to stop if we want to reach the level of recovery needed to remain clean and sober long-term.

It's also quite possible to tell the truth and not give much information. For example, if someone you don't know well asks you a personal question, you don't have to answer it, but you don't have to lie, either. Simply telling the person, "That's too personal for me to discuss" is an honest and straightforward answer. Honesty is one of the pillars of assertive communication, which we'll get into later.

Other ways to be honest include following through on

promises, owning up to your mistakes when you make them, and expressing your true feelings. If there are people you've lied to in the past, you may want to come clean to them, but please consult with a sponsor or therapist first. Or, at the very least, read the chapter on step nine to determine if coming clean is a good idea or whether it could be potentially harmful.

Humility

Humility is a character trait that is primarily demonstrated by how you relate to others. Humility is the antidote to the poisons known as arrogance and entitlement. Practicing humility can begin by talking less about yourself, especially if you often boast or brag. Instead, ask people about themselves. Be genuinely curious. Stay silent when you feel an intense urge to jump into a conversation and discuss your own opinion. Practice acting like a person who understands they are no more or less valuable than anyone else.

Humility does not mean putting yourself down or acting less valuable than others. It's about adjusting your ego to a realistic size. It's not about acting like a king or a peasant. You're trying to become a man among men, a woman among women, a human among other humans. Yes, there may be things you're better at than others, but take the time to notice the things that other people do better than you do. Give genuine compliments. Learn to notice and appreciate the gifts that others possess. Realize that it's not all about you.

Skepticism

The word "skepticism" gets a really bad rap. People often confuse skepticism with cynicism, which is a mindset in which one assumes the worst about people and their intentions. It's actually quite different. Skepticism is a healthy quality that helps combat cockiness and stubbornness. It's the willingness to engage in critical thinking and challenge any belief by looking at the evidence to support or refute it. In the 12-step world, faith is often sold as a virtue necessary for recovery. I think there is a place for trust, confidence, and hope, but faith implies believing something without evidence, which I have yet to be convinced is a good thing. Instead, I prefer skepticism, which means healthy doubt about your own beliefs as well as the beliefs of others.

I often think of skepticism as a close cousin of humility. It takes a certain level of humility to be willing to acknowledge that you don't know everything. It feels good to feel like you have the right information and the right view on a given topic. While it's true that you might, it's important to always be open to new information. It's one thing to be confident in your beliefs, but it's quite another to be *certain* of your beliefs. One leaves room for growth and the other does not. It's perfectly OK to be confident in your viewpoints when they are substantiated with evidence. For example, as you'll find later in this book, I believe mindfulness to be one of the most powerful tools available for improving mental health. This belief comes not just from personal experience, but from the abundance of scientific evidence to support it. However, if some irrefutable proof were presented to me showing that mindfulness doesn't work, I would have to be willing to change my belief.

One way you can exercise your skeptic muscle is by speaking in a more careful manner. Saying things like, "I might be wrong, but…" or "Based on what I've seen, I believe…" shows that you are always open to the possibility that there may be information you don't have. In addition to speaking carefully, practice thinking critically about things from multiple perspectives and always asking yourself, "could I be wrong?" Replace concepts like "always" and "never" with "often" and "rarely." There are very, very few absolutes in this world. As my old sponsor would say, "Even black and white movies aren't black and white." Skepticism is an essential trait for anyone trying to live a humble, honest, reality-based life.

Generosity

Generosity is one of the simplest (not easiest) character traits to develop. All it requires is regular acts of generosity. No big mystery. However, the first thing that comes to people's minds when they think of generosity is the giving of material possessions. While this is certainly an option if you can do it without causing yourself undue hardship, it is by no means the only way to be generous. I like to consider kindness a type of generosity that involves giving of yourself and your time rather than money or material goods. Holding a door open, helping someone carry groceries, picking up trash that isn't yours, doing something nice for someone for no reason at all, or doing extra chores around the house to make your roommate's lives easier. There are ample opportunities throughout the day to practice generosity. It's one of the easiest things to plan for, so make a plan to perform at least one generous act a day. It doesn't have to be huge. A little goes a long way.

When you start practicing generosity more often, you'll likely begin to notice that you *seek* opportunities to practice it. Generosity is tremendously rewarding. It's as if there is some innate human desire to give of yourself both emotionally and materially. As with all things, though, try to keep this in balance. Some people focus on helping others for the wrong reasons: either because they want to influence the relationship or because they feel guilty if they put themselves before another person. True generosity comes from a place of confidence and authenticity, and can only truly occur when you have your basic needs met. There are no ulterior motives or expectations for something in return. It is not being done to avoid guilt or shame. If you notice yourself doing for others out of fear, obligation, or the expectation of getting something in return, you may need to get honest with yourself about what is driving this. Sometimes, generosity can be a disguise for manipulation, entitlement, or guilt.

Assertiveness

Not to be confused with aggressiveness, assertiveness is saying what you mean with confidence and clarity. Aggression is operating from a place of hostility and anger, while assertiveness is operating from a place of honesty and directness. You can be assertive and still be perfectly cordial and polite. For example, if someone asks you to pass the breadsticks but you can't reach them, it is assertive to say, "I can't reach them right now." Aggression would be reaching across the table, grabbing a breadstick, and throwing it at the asker's head. We generally want to avoid assault with baked goods at this stage of our recovery, so we stick with assertiveness whenever possible.

Assertiveness is crucial if we want to feel empowered and in control of our lives. I cannot stress how important it is, for example, to be able to set limits and boundaries with people when they do something you are not OK with. When people are not assertive, they end up being passive or aggressive (or passive-aggressive). Being passive leads to anxiety, frustration, and resentment, while aggression pushes people away and can destroy relationships and potentially even land you in legal trouble. In addition, aggression doesn't really solve the underlying issue. It gets a short-term result at the expense of the relationship.

Let's say a friend insults you. You can respond passively by saying nothing or laughing nervously, you can respond aggressively by yelling or being violent, or you can respond assertively by saying, "That went too far, I don't appreciate that." Of all three, assertiveness is almost always the best choice. It doesn't always mean the other person will respect it, but it provides the best chances of resulting in a mutual understanding and allowing the relationship to grow from the miscommunication. If you're assertive with someone and they don't respect it, that's an important factor to consider when determining what (if any) role you want this person to play in your life.

Responsibility

Over my years of watching people grow in life and in recovery, I have not seen a single shift in mentality that is more transformative than the shift from placing blame to accepting responsibility. It is common for addicts to look for the fault in others that has "made" them behave a certain way. They may complain about how their job "makes them" drink, or their spouse "makes them" want to get high. There is no better way to stay stuck than to believe other people are at fault for making you act a certain way. If that's the case, your only hope of changing is to change the behaviors of everyone around you, and then you're screwed.

As mentioned in the section on step four, taking responsibility for our behaviors does not mean we are saying other people aren't ever wrong. It's perfectly fine to acknowledge that you were wronged and process your feelings about that, but if you use that as an excuse to behave a certain way, you are committing to a victim mentality. Even if you were a victim of something, you are now responsible for your healing and for how you respond to what happened. If you were abused as a child, you are by no means at fault and you didn't do anything wrong. However, if you use that as justification for mistreating yourself or others, you've neglected to take responsibility for your present life.

Compassion

Being compassionate is important for multiple reasons. For one, it vastly improves your personal relationships. Nothing can de-escalate a conflict faster than demonstrating an understanding of the other person's point of view. Secondly, it makes it all that much easier to understand others and let go of anger or judgment toward them. Once you take some time to comprehend someone's behavior, it is much easier to cut them a little slack. It also frees you from the unpleasant experience of feeling judgment towards someone.

Empathy is important as well, but not necessarily helpful on its own. It's possible to have empathy without compassion. Empathy is feeling another person's feelings, which can just be unpleasant and draining on its own. However, when we use our sense of empathy to develop more of a logical understanding of someone's plight, we are practicing compassion[9]. Compassion tends to produce a desire to be helpful, while empathy itself doesn't always lead to motivation to act.

Compassion can be practiced by pausing when you're feeling judgmental and taking a few seconds to consider what the other person is experiencing that may be contributing to their behavior. If your spouse is yelling at you for not doing the dishes, you can take a moment to consider where the yelling is coming from. Perhaps he had a particularly hard day at work and is tired. Perhaps he has told you yesterday that he wants help with the dishes and is now feeling unheard. Whatever the case may be, approaching the situation compassionately is much less likely to lead to a fight and far more likely to give the other person space to look at his or her own part in the conflict.

Self-Care

There are countless books and articles out there on self-care. It is such an important part of recovery and living a healthy life that I've added a separate section about it after the steps. It honestly needs its own book to be adequately addressed, but that's not what this book is about, so I'm just going to scratch the surface.

Just about any unhealthy character trait can be made worse by a lack of self-care. If you're naturally an impatient person, you're going to be extra impatient if you didn't get enough sleep. If you're naturally a selfish person, you'll be much less inclined to consider others if you're stressed from overworking. Lack of self-care is an epidemic in Western society. We've somehow come to believe that working ourselves to the bone and being constantly busy is the right thing to do. Self-care is often seen as a luxury reserved only for retirees, children, and lazy folk. Nothing could be farther from the truth.

Self-care needs to be at the top of our priority list. It is what allows us to sustain our ability to work, care for a family, go to school, learn a new skill, do chores, maintain relationships, etc. If you put any of those goals ahead of self-care, your mood, mental health, and the goals themselves will start to suffer. You'll begin to compensate for the lack of self-care by increasing your use of unhealthy coping skills such as overeating, smoking, avoidance, aggression, and isolating from others. It is simply impossible to function long-term in a demanding world without taking some time to regularly focus on your own needs.

Increase your self-care by finding just one new habit to start incorporating into your daily life. It doesn't matter how small it is; we have to start somewhere. Even if it's as simple as taking a bath at night or taking ten minutes to read before bed, a little self-care will go a long way. In addition, one of the most vital forms of self-care is exercise. You must exercise. *Everyone* needs to exercise. Our bodies and minds to not function optimally without regular physical activity, and just as with other forms of self-care, a little can go a long way. Start with walking for 20 minutes 2-3 times a week. Once a new habit becomes ingrained, add another one until you feel like your needs are being reasonably met. In my experience, people need at least an hour of self-care per day to feel sane. Some forms of self-care include reading, hobbies, exercising, socializing, meditating, viewing entertainment, being creative, and so on.

Step seven is never fully complete. It's something you will be striving to do on a regular basis for as long as you feel the need to build your character. If you are regularly engaging in some of your healthy behaviors and growing your goal traits, then you can feel free to move forward with the steps. The practical version of step seven is much more of a long-term process than the original version. When you feel like you are solid in your regular step seven activities, you can move on to your last (I promise) list: step eight.

Step Eight

AA Version

Made a list of all persons we had harmed and became willing to make amends to them all

Practical Version

Determined the best way to make amends to those we had harmed

The only real difference between the classic version of this step and the practical version is that the practical version doesn't include anything about willingness. For one, we can assume you have *some* willingness to make amends to the people you've harmed, otherwise you wouldn't be embarking on this process. You may not be willing to make amends to them all yet, and that's OK. You don't need to be willing to make amends to everyone in order to make amends to your first person. Start with that, and as you move along in your amends process, you will likely start to let go of any resistance you have to some of your more difficult amends. I'll address this in the section about step nine.

There are a few options when it comes to the details of this step. One of my sponsors had me write a standard list while another sponsor had me use flash cards for each individual I had to make amends to. At the end of the day, I don't think it matters much. Pick a method that works for you and makes it easy for you to keep track of the person and how you plan to make amends to them. I found the flashcards to be my favorite because I could write notes on it and bring it with me when I was about to make my amends. It helped me to give it a quick look and refresh my memory before meeting with the person I was making my amends to.

Working Step Eight

This step is quite straightforward. Refer to your list of all the people you've harmed. You wrote it in step four. For each one, consider the harm you caused and how you might be able to make it right. Remember that making amends is not about saying you're sorry, it's about repairing the damage you caused as thoroughly as you can. For example, if you stole a car, making amends is more than finding the victim and saying, "hey, sorry about stealing your car that one time." An amends for something like that would be more along the lines of repaying the value of the car over a period of time as well as not stealing any more cars. As the instructions for step nine will illustrate, our idea of how to make amends may change once we interact with the person we hurt. It's also possible that we will never actually get a chance to make the amends directly. For now, we will take our best guess as to how we can best make things right with each person.

When it comes to choosing the "best" way to make amends, we need to look at a few factors. For one, is this amends addressing the actual damage that we caused? Is the damage we caused financial, emotional, physical, or a combination? It's crucial to make sure that we address all potential areas of harm. It's a very deflating experience to make your amends and then later realize there was more you should have addressed. Also, is your amends something you can actually do, or is it potentially going to cause you undue hardship? If so, it may be worth it to explore ways that you can make the amends effectively without putting an excessive burden on yourself. Some burden is appropriate, but you still need to live your life.

Make sure you take the time to consider if the person

you owe amends to will potentially be harmed by the amends process. For example, if you seriously hurt somebody either through violence, sexual assault, or other forms of abuse, be exceedingly careful when planning to make amends to them. If your actions resulted in someone's trauma, the last thing you want to do is cause that person to re-experience the emotions associated with that trauma by contacting them inappropriately. It is not OK to relieve yourself of guilt at the expense of another person. Also, if a person you previously harmed has explicitly stated that they do not want you to contact them ever again, then you would be causing more harm by contacting them. If you think someone might be harmed by your amends, run it by another person in recovery. If you ultimately decide the amends is inappropriate, look into making a living amends. I'll explain what that is in the next section.

Once we've determined the best way to make amends to the people we've harmed, we move on to step nine and begin the actual process of making the amends.

Step Nine

AA Version

Made direct amends to such people wherever possible, except when to do so would injure them or others

Practical Version

Made direct amends to such people wherever possible, except when to do so would cause harm

Making amends is about doing the right thing so that we can become people of integrity and clearing our conscience of guilt and shame so that we can walk around feeling free and unburdened by our past. It's about healing ourselves just as much as it's about repairing the damage we've inflicted on others. Sometimes, our amends will lead to renewed relationships with old friends and acquaintances, and sometimes it won't. At the end of the day, what's important is that you've cleaned up your side of the street and can go to sleep knowing you did all you could to remedy the damage you caused in the past.

There's not much about step nine that needs to be changed from the original version. My only change involves using the word "harm" instead of "injure." Also, I suggest avoiding making the amends if it causes harm to *anyone*, including yourself. We are not doing this process to harm ourselves; we are doing it to improve our lives. We will certainly feel uncomfortable during parts of this process, but that is not the same thing as doing something that is self-destructive.

The first portion of this step states to make direct (meaning face-to-face) amends "wherever possible."

Obviously, there will be situations where making amends directly is impossible. The person we harmed may be deceased, impossible to locate, or someone whose identity you don't remember. It could also be a general harm to lots of people (e.g. being rude to restaurant servers for 20 years), in which case making a direct amends to hundreds of servers is probably not practical. For these amends, we do what are called "living amends," which are essentially changes to the ways we interact in the world that "make up for" our harms.

The second portion of this step states that we don't make an amends (or choose a different kind to make) if it is going to cause harm. When I use the term, "harm," I'm referring to something that has an overall negative impact. The best way to avoid this is to ask the person you plan on making amends to whether or not they are open to it. If they are, then they are probably willing to experience some level of discomfort, which I don't consider a harm worthy of skipping an amends.

It's also important not to harm yourself during this process. The vast majority of the time, this will not be something you need to worry about. On rare occasions, however, an amends may cause you more harm than good. For example, some folks in the 12-step world will suggest actually putting yourself at risk of jail or prison time if necessary. The wisdom of this approach is highly debatable.

If the risk of you doing time as a result of your amends is low, then I usually suggest doing it. For example, if you make amends to a neighbor for stealing and offer to pay them back, the chances of them pressing charges is pretty low, so I would suggest making that amends. If, on the other hand, you did something like vandalize a public place, I would not consider it wise to turn yourself in to supposedly pay your debt to society. You can do more overall good by volunteering for community service or otherwise helping someone in need. I strongly doubt going to jail or prison really makes anything right. It's more often purely a punishment that can cause lasting damage[10]. This is infinitely more true if you have a family that you need to be present for. Prison is useful for protecting society from actively destructive people, but, thanks to this path you're on, that's not who you are anymore. That being said, if you truly feel that spending time in the can is a debt you need to pay to feel fully free, then you have my blessing. Ultimately, how you choose to deal with amends that may get you in trouble is something you'll have to decide on a case-by-case basis with your sponsor or a therapist.

Working Step Nine

This step is all about getting out into the world and making things right. Even though it makes a great premise for a sitcom, the truth is that this can be a scary and intimidating process. It's normal and healthy for you to feel a little freaked out at the idea of facing people you've harmed. The good news is that you only have to make the amends one at a time. Don't think about your entire list; just focus on the next one. A fellow addict taught me an approach to this step that I found very useful for people who are feeling highly resistant to the process. He suggested sorting your amends into three groups. One group is the "ready" group, the second is the "maybe" group, and the third is the "never" group. People who you are ready to make amends to go in the "ready" group, people you're unsure about go in the "maybe" group, and people you damn sure never want to go near are in the "never" group. The idea is that, as you work your way through the first and second group, you will likely be ready when it comes time to make amends to the people in your "never" group.

Making direct amends is simple enough. Contact the person to whom you want to make amends, either by phone or email, let them know that you are working a program to better yourself, and offer to make things right. If the person agrees, meet them somewhere semi-private and carry out the amends. If they don't want to meet you face-to-face, respect their decision. Make your amends as outlined in your 8th step. The person may respond well to your amends or they may not. Regardless, do not get defensive or make excuses. Do your best to listen and understand where they are coming from. End the amends by letting the person know that you are open to hearing if there is any harm you inflicted that you left out of your amends. If they have any, listen intently and validate them. If they have specific requests of you such as paying back money or providing a service to make things right, you don't have to answer on the spot. You can tell them that you'll get back to them later with an answer. Once the amends is finished, politely get the heck out of there. Hanging around after an amends can sometimes ruin an otherwise successful process. If the person you made amends to wants to spend more time with you later on, they'll let you know.

While it doesn't happen often, an amends can sometimes go awry. The person may become angry, aggressive, and in *very* rare cases, violent. I've never experienced this. The worst story I've ever heard about was a father getting slapped by his daughter during the amends process. Even with that, it ended well and they rebuilt their relationship. There is very little need to worry about being physically harmed during this process. That being said, anything can happen, and you are *not* doing this to be punished or abused. If someone crosses the line while you are making the amends, you have every right to excuse yourself and leave. This is extremely rare, but know that it's an acceptable option if necessary. You can consider your side of the street clean for trying.

Some of these amends will be impossible to make directly. For these, I'm a fan of living amends. A living amends is the act of making things right by making changes to the way you live. We practice engaging in a reparative behavior until we feel we have rectified our harm. For example, if you abused a pet that is no longer living, you can obviously not make amends to that pet, so you may consider volunteering some time at an animal shelter or being exceptionally kind to your current pet (if you have one). If you stole from a stranger you'll never be able to locate, you may consider donating some money or material goods to charity along with vowing to never steal again. The idea is to regularly engage in behavior that in some way counters the suffering that your harmful actions caused. If you can't counter the suffering, at the very least you are pledging to not cause more.

As with many of the steps, you may never fully "finish" this one. New memories of past harms will likely pop into your head for many years. For this reason, we have the next three steps, which are often considered the "maintenance" steps. These steps essentially involve revisiting the previous steps informally and re-working parts of them as necessary. Once you feel you've made all the direct amends you can at the moment, you are ready to move on to step ten.

Step Ten

AA Version

Continued to take personal inventory, and when we were wrong, promptly admitted it

Practical Version

Practiced daily self-reflection and continued making amends whenever necessary

Every step has the potential to be powerful, but nothing has transformed my life and relationships as profoundly as step ten. For this step, you make a concerted effort to stay mindful of your own behaviors throughout your daily interactions. Even if you feel you've been wronged, take the time to look at where you could have done things differently. If you determine that you made a mistake, own up to it as quickly as possible. It may be helpful to have a nightly routine where you sit down and contemplate your day. You can use this time to take note of any instances where you may have caused harm. If any occur to you, jot them down and make amends for them as soon as you can.

If you dedicate yourself to making this step an integral part of your life, you will be astonished at how much your life improves. You will experience the incredible lightness that comes from ending each day knowing that you kept your side of the street clean. Next time you get into an argument with a co-worker, friend, or family member, practice acknowledging your part in the conflict. It is astoundingly effective at de-escalating the situation and allowing for a positive resolution. Some people worry that admitting your faults makes you appear weak. I beg to differ. Owning your mistakes takes a strength and confidence that most healthy people respect.

Working Step Ten

Some people prefer to do this step in a structured manner, while others simply stay mindful of their behavior throughout their day. It might help if you do a little writing each day at first until the self-reflection becomes more automatic. If you do decide to do some writing, you can do it in the style of the step four tables or you can simply journal. Journaling is a very powerful tool that I consider an essential component of self-reflection. Writing about your behavior is an excellent way to gain some perspective on it and possibly notice patterns you may have glossed over otherwise.

At the very least, start to take moments throughout the day to pause and think back on how you've interacted with others. You might consider setting a daily alarm on your phone to remind you to take a moment. It doesn't have to be any more than a minute. Sit quietly and consider any possible instances throughout the day where you might have caused harm. If any come to mind, think about how you can make it right.

You don't have to get obsessive about this. I'm not suggesting that you go back to every single person you think you may have slighted in some vague manner during the day and apologize to them. If it's a small harm, just make note of it and try not to do it again. The goal is not to feel a constant pressure to be perfect. Instead, you're just making a habit of bringing a little awareness to your daily life that you might not have had before. With step ten, things that have previously gone unnoticed may be noticed, which gives you the opportunity to try something different if you so choose.

Remember that step ten is a maintenance step. It's not something you do in one sitting before moving on to step eleven. It's a new habit you're practicing on a daily basis. That may sound like a lot when heaped on to the other daily practices we've been discussing, but it ultimately amounts to another minute or two per day where you practice pausing and thinking about your interactions during the day. The best thing about this step is that the more you do it, the less you need to do it. As you become increasingly aware of your less-than-ideal behaviors, you will get better at preventing them in the first place, which is a win for you and everyone you come in contact with.

Step Eleven

AA Version

Sought through prayer and meditation to improve our conscious contact with God as we understood Him, praying only for knowledge of His will for us and the power to carry that out

Practical Version

We started meditating

Throughout this process, you'll discover—if you haven't already—that none of these steps exists in a vacuum. They all impact each other and are impacted by the others. This is particularly true for step eleven. The ultimate goal of this step is to engage regularly in the practice of mindfulness, which has been demonstrated time and again to benefit multiple areas of one's mental health. Being mindful means being consciously aware of something (usually breath, bodily sensations, or thoughts) without judgment or resistance. The best way to practice this is through meditation, but it can be practiced throughout the day as well. I recommend utilizing both for optimal results.

There's a reason that dozens of books (maybe even hundreds, I didn't count) specifically about mindfulness meditation have been written in recent years. Western civilization is catching on to an ancient practice that has the power to relieve anxiety, improve patience, increase insight, reduce aggression, increase impulse control, improve sleep, and more[11]. If it sounds too good to be true, that's because there's a catch: it's not exciting—at least not at first. Initially, practicing mindfulness meditation feels weird and unnatural, and that's because, for many of us, it is. The last thing our racing minds want is for us to be in the moment. Our minds want us drinking, smoking, worrying, watching TV, playing video games, socializing, working, sleeping, etc. Mindfulness meditation flies right in the face of our mind's baser instincts and forces us to step out of the raging current that is our thoughts.

In the original version of this step, meditation is seen as a way to improve your conscious contact with God, thus helping you get in touch with what God's "will" is for you. Obviously, that is not what the practical version is about. The results are similar, but I'm obviously chalking them up to a psychological change rather than divine intervention. While you probably won't hear the voice of the creator of the Universe, regular mindfulness meditation can help you develop your intuition: that "gut" feeling you get that tells you what to do in a given situation. It is my personal belief that this is what the more religious members of 12-step programs are calling "God." Unfortunately, assigning this phenomenon to a deity further promotes the idea that we are not capable of making wise, healthy choices without the help of a divine being. I have a more empowering take: we can sharpen and refine our insight and intuition by engaging in a practice that helps us think clearly and efficiently without being overwhelmed by our emotions or repetitive thoughts.

Our brains are phenomenally complex organs. It truly is mind-boggling to consider just how much is happening in there. We take in sensory input, analyze it, and respond to it in fractions of a second. We're capable of making memories, problem solving, projecting into the future, intuiting the emotions of others, and creating fantasies. When it comes to the incredible things our brains can do, the list is practically endless. That being said, we also have areas of our brain that are, to put it bluntly, pretty stupid in comparison. Primarily, these are older parts of our brain such as the brain stem, often referred to as our "reptilian brain" and the limbic system, which includes the amygdala (fight-or-flight response), hypothalamus (hormone regulation), hippocampus (memory), in addition to multiple other structures that it would take a textbook to explain in detail. The point is that these "lower" parts of our brain, when activated by stress or anxiety, can often override the "higher" parts of our brain involved in critical thinking, planning, and working memory[12].

Our fight-or-flight response did us a lot of good way back when running away from lions, tigers, and bears was a common occurrence and a high priority. We would perceive a threat, our amygdala would tell our hypothalamus to activate our sympathetic nervous system (heavy breathing, rapid heartbeat, increased blood flow) and we would either fight the threat or get the heck outta Dodge[13]. Nowadays, however, our brain mistakes perceived threats such as work deadlines, social rejection, worst-case scenario fantasies, and the expectations of others for current threats to our well-being. The end result is that many of us are in a near-constant state of fight-or-flight. In turn, our more rational brain is compromised and we make more impulsive decisions, struggle to regulate our emotions, and seek external means of soothing ourselves (drugs, sex, junk food, TV, etc.)

This is all a bit of an oversimplification, but the moral of the story is that we need to spend more time residing in our higher brain and less time residing in our lower brain. And how do we do that? By exercising our higher brain. As a result of doing this regularly, we will still be able to notice and acknowledge our raw emotions and impulses (in fact, we'll become even more aware of them), but we will not immediately react to them or take them as seriously as we did before. We'll be able to observe the more automatic parts of our mind from a distance. This doesn't mean that we're suppressing or avoiding them, we just aren't letting them *become* us. This will make more sense as you practice. If you've never meditated before, this may all sound like airy-fairy nonsense, and that's OK. Give it a try and you'll get to experience it yourself.

Although it may seem like I'm disparaging human emotions, that's not my intention. Our emotions are extremely important and can give us good insight into what's going on with us and what actions we need to take in response. The problem is that our emotions often have far too much control over how we ultimately decide to behave. We aren't looking to separate ourselves from emotions, but rather to manage them gracefully and give them a healthier role in our lives. When we feel anger, it's often a sign that someone is mistreating us. If we are mindful, we can notice the anger and make a decision to address the problem. If we aren't mindful, our anger may turn to rage and cause us to engage in impulsive, destructive behavior that only makes the situation worse. Emotions have a necessary place in our lives; they aren't "good" or "bad." Emotions are *information* that tell us something about what we need. The damage occurs when we act solely based on emotions rather than observing them and using the higher functions of our brain to decide how to manage them.

The results of regular meditation differ depending on how often you do it, how much you've done it in the past, how stressed you are, your temperament, and several other factors. Some people report that a meditation practice is nothing short of life changing, while others report results that are still positive, but less dramatic. One of my favorite books on this subject is *10% Happier* by Dan Harris. In it, he describes his life as a news anchor and the regular stress that led to an eventual panic attack live on the air. This incident motivated him to find a solution to his anxiety, and he discovered mindfulness meditation. The book is titled as such because Harris claims that this regular practice hasn't necessarily revolutionized his life, but has made him 10% happier, which he considers worth the effort. He also has a podcast named after the book which I highly suggest you take a listen to.

It's clear that meditation is helpful for just about everyone, but why is it that it's one of the tools recommended specifically for recovering addicts? If you recall the earlier chapter on addiction, a major factor in our compulsive behavior is the sub- or semi-conscious desire to soothe ourselves due to a persistent state of discomfort or unease. Through mindfulness meditation, we become more aware of this underlying sense of discomfort and actually begin to desensitise ourselves to it. Much as a person with a snake phobia gets better from being gradually exposed to snakes, we are practicing sitting in and accepting our general feeling of discontent. The paradoxical effect of accepting it and exposing ourselves to it is that it tends to get better and can even vanish completely. While I know that sounds great, be careful of developing expectations. It may happen or it may not. Acceptance is about not having your own agenda, but accepting everything as it is *now*.

Working Step Eleven

The instructions are in the step itself. For this step, all you have to do is meditate. There are several different forms of meditation, and all of them can be beneficial. However, the form of meditation that has the most current research behind it is mindfulness meditation. This chapter will be a crash course that should be enough to get you started, but there is much, much more to learn if you want. As I said before, there are countless books available on the subject. In addition, there are guided meditations all over the Internet that allow you to jump right in without any previous experience. One of my favorite sites is marc.ucla.edu. It's the website for the Mindful Awareness Research Center at UCLA. They offer quite a few guided meditations that you can listen to for free on their website. There is absolutely no religiosity or supernatural belief incorporated into them.

When it comes to meditation, the truth is that more is almost always better. The more you meditate, the more tuned-in you will be to your inner world and the thoughts and feelings that drive you. That being said, we all have lives and limited time. Ideally, you should be meditating daily for 15-20 minutes. Some people report twenty minutes twice a day as being particularly effective. At the moment, that amount of time sitting still might sound excruciating to you, so meditate for as long as you are able to. I do suggest, however, that you pick a time beforehand and stick to it, even if it's just two minutes. If you don't have a timer set, you'll struggle to meditate because you'll be too busy wondering how long you've been meditating.

The classic image of a person meditating is that of a robed monk sitting in the full lotus position on a round cushion (called a zafu), arms out with forearms vertical, making a strange gesture with his hands and reciting a mantra or humming. You can certainly do this if you're so inclined, but I'm happy to say it isn't necessary. All you need is a comfortable place to sit and a timer. Some meditators like sitting on the floor, while others (such as myself) are a bit too inflexible to sit in that position for long. If that's you, a chair is more than OK. Some people even prefer walking meditation, which I won't cover here, but can often be just as powerful as sitting meditation. A quick Google search will give you plenty of info to get started if you want to pursue that. However, I'd still recommend starting with seated meditation to keep things simple at first.

To begin, sit with your back straight and your head in a comfortable position, not too far forward or too far back. You want to be relaxed, but not so relaxed that you'll fall asleep. Don't lean back in your chair or slouch. Contrary to popular belief, meditation is not a passive practice, it is quite active and requires you to be alert and focused. After you're seated, start your timer, close your eyes, and focus your attention on your breath. Don't change your breathing intentionally; just observe it. Pick a few sensations to focus on, such as your chest rising and falling or the cool sensation of air entering your nostrils. Do your best to focus all of your attention on nothing but your breathing. If you're able to do this for more than a second or two without your mind wandering, I am in awe of your skills.

While you're meditating, your mind *will* wander. Another common misconception about meditation is that "successful" meditation should result in a "clear mind," or a mind with no thoughts. The truth of the matter is that this experience is extremely rare, especially for beginners. As I said before, our mind does not want to stay still; it wants to jump around and make a lot of noise, which is why it is often referred to by mindfulness practitioners as the "monkey mind." Do not be discouraged when your mind wanders. That is an *essential* part of meditation and something even the most advanced practitioners experience. All you need to do when this occurs is notice that you've been distracted and direct your attention back to the breath.

Every time you direct your attention back to the breath, think of it as lifting a weight. Each time you do it, your attention muscle is getting a little bit stronger. You are getting a little more practice at staying in the moment despite your mind's relentless efforts to pull you away from the here and now. This will happen a lot in the first few minutes of meditation, and will slowly quiet down as your session progresses. Some days you might notice very few thoughts, while other days you'll feel like there is no hope of ever shutting your mind up. All veteran meditators have experienced both ends of the spectrum many, many times. Don't give up. If you happen to get to a point where you are truly free of thought, congratulations! You've reached enlightenment. Please write a book because I want to read it.

As you get a little more comfortable meditating, you can also try labeling your distractions briefly before turning your attention back to your breath. For example, if you find yourself worrying about an upcoming job interview, you can just gently label it "worry" in your mind and then refocus your attention. It's probably best to wait until you're somewhat experienced with focusing only on the breath before you incorporate labeling. When you do incorporate it, however, you'll likely find that it's a useful tool when it comes to learning more about your thought patterns. You may notice that you think about your social life way more than you thought you did, or you may find that 99.99% of your thoughts are self-centered, or you may just notice that you're a judgmental a-hole. Regardless, if you spend a good deal of time observing the circus that is your thinking, it's going to be darn near impossible to not learn a few things about yourself. If those things happen to be things you don't like, we already know how to start changing them (hint: steps six and seven).

Any amount of meditation will be beneficial in some way. Some is always better than none. With that being said, I *strongly* encourage you to try and do more. Many people report that they don't even feel fully "in" their meditation until they've hit the 20-minute mark. Even if you don't do it daily, pick one day a week where you take the time to do a long meditation session. There are significant changes that occur in your subjective experience after a sustained period of focused attention. The longer you do it, the more you'll be able to notice some of the subtler thoughts that creep their way into your consciousness. You may remember things you haven't thought of in years or have deep realizations about the way your mind works. You get out what you put in. If you meditate one minute a day, you'll get some benefits, but you'll only get one minute a day's worth.

As you get better and better at meditation, you may find yourself wanting to venture into more advanced techniques or other forms of meditation such as loving-kindness or metta, which is excellent for developing compassion. Mindfulness meditation also has its own progression. Practitioners traditionally start with the breath as a focal point and then eventually move on to focusing on bodily sensations, thoughts, and finally our entire field of awareness. If you take a liking to this meditation thing, there are multiple ways to explore it further such as joining meditation groups, retreats, and even smartphone apps.

You may also be wondering, "can't I just forget all this silliness and listen to music with my eyes closed?" Sure you can. You're not meditating "incorrectly" if you use meditation specifically to relax and calm yourself down. Sometimes we just don't have it in us to focus for extended periods of time on a single stimulus. If you're feeling resistant to mindfulness meditation, by all means, grab a pair of headphones and listen to some music in a dark room or head on over to myNoise.net (I have no financial connection with that site, it's just plain awesome) and listen to different ambient sounds while you sit quietly. Just don't give up on mindfulness completely. While relaxation has many benefits, the specific practice of mindfulness offers unique benefits that may not be as easily obtained by other means.

Needless to say, this topic can get pretty in-depth and complicated. The basics, however, are very simple and straightforward: find a time each day to sit down and practice mindfulness meditation for anywhere from a minute to an hour. The more time you dedicate to it, the more benefits you'll see. In addition, regular practice will result in longer-lasting changes. If you meditate today, you may feel different today, but if you meditate every day for several weeks, months, or years, you'll likely notice lasting changes that persist outside of active meditation. Meditation can lead to altered *states*, while a long-term meditation practice can lead to altered *traits* such as increased calmness, improved emotional regulation, and a mental shift in regards to how one relates to thoughts and feeling[14]. Altered states are delightful, but what we're ultimately after in recovery (and in life) is altered traits that stick with us and improve our life and the lives of those around us.

It's time to move on to step twelve. But first, sit down and meditate.

Step Twelve

AA Version

Having had a spiritual awakening as the result of these steps, we tried to carry this message to alcoholics and to practice these principles in all our affairs

Practical Version

Sought to retain our newfound recovery lifestyle by teaching it to those willing to learn and by surrounding ourselves with healthy people

The AA version of this step and the practical version share the same basic principle: to help others as a means of further enforcing what you've learned. The practical version doesn't mention anything about practicing these principles in all of our affairs because that has been implied since the beginning. We are not building this new lifestyle in order to be sober for a short period of time and then revert back to our old ways. It goes without saying that, if we've made it this far, we're in it for the long haul. This is also not just something we're doing when we're around other people or for show. We're living this new lifestyle so that we can be happier, and more at ease with ourselves.

The reason we help others is threefold. For one, it reinforces the lessons that we've learned. Nothing reminds you to practice honesty in your life like showing others how to do it themselves. It's a very awkward experience to be regularly teaching people to practice their goal traits when you are actively engaging in your unhealthy traits. Not that it's impossible—there are plenty of walking contradictions who don't practice what they preach, but it's unlikely that that's sustainable. For the most part, if you are genuinely helping others, you are going to be more motivated to do it yourself.

Secondly, we help others because it can provide us with a sense of meaning unlike anything else. When you see someone come into a meeting stumbling drunk (or high) and you reach out your hand to help, you will feel a buzz far greater than any substance when you see that person slowly come back to life over time thanks in part to the compassion and guidance that you have given them. It will reinforce your commitment to building and maintaining a recovery lifestyle when you see it happen for someone else.

Thirdly, we help others because it is just the right thing to do. There are countless people in the world suffering from behavioral and substance addictions. If you find a solution that works, how does it make sense to keep it to yourself? Again, I'm not suggesting that you go proselytizing to people sitting in bars, but there are plenty of places to go where you can find people who are willing to try something new. Your experience and knowledge will be welcome there, and it is desperately needed. We'll get more into specifically how to start this process in the next section.

The final part of this step emphasizes surrounding ourselves with healthy people. This is absolutely crucial and honestly something that should start on day one. In this step, however, we are going to be taking some more specific actions towards really making it happen. As I stated earlier in the book, there is simply no plausible way to maintain a lifestyle of recovery if you are surrounded by people who are still engaging in self-destructive behavior. That's not to say that everyone in your life needs to be a saint, or even completely sober, but they need to be non-toxic, which is another subject that I will touch on later.

Working Step Twelve

Spreading the message is great, but don't go to your local promenade with a megaphone and start preaching this stuff. That's not what this step is suggesting. The goal is not to become a self-righteous proselytizer, but to instead be a model of mental health who can be trusted to provide valuable guidance to those in need. We aren't going to just sit back and wait for people to come to us, but we also aren't going to go on a mad hunt for drunks and addicts that have no desire to change. As with all other areas of our recovery, we are looking for a more balanced and reasonable approach.

The most efficient way to find people to help, without question, is to look for them in 12-step meetings. In-person 12-step meetings are where most addicts seeking help end up, and they are everywhere. All you have to do is go to a meeting regularly and talk to the newcomers. You don't even need to offer to sponsor them. All you need to do is be there, answer their questions, and provide guidance if they seem ready. Being a welcoming presence to someone who is afraid and confused about the process can be hugely impactful. At the first meeting I attended, one of the greeters was an exceptionally friendly and calming person to be around. He immediately helped me feel at ease. Were it not for him, it's entirely possible I would have shied away from meetings and either delayed my sobriety or not gotten sober at all.

If you live in a place where there aren't a lot of meetings, you can always find phone meetings and/or online forums where you can share what you've learned. There are online communities such as Reddit where people from all walks of life gather to discuss common interests. Subreddits are subsections of Reddit dedicated to a specific topic. Subreddits such as r/stopdrinking, r/alcoholism, r/SoberLifeProTips, and r/sober are potential places to start. Just know that people in these online communities will probably not take kindly to someone coming in and preaching, so stick with offering assistance only when it is solicited. It's also important to understand that some people have been so badly burned by their initial 12-step experiences that they will not be open to hearing anything even remotely close to a 12-step approach, even if it is secular.

It may be wise to look specifically for meetings or communities that already lean towards being non-religious. If you can't find such a place (atheist and agnostic meetings do exist, but are rare), then it's important not to assume the person you are trying to help is going to be best served by a more rational approach to the steps. Faith is powerful and it may be extremely motivating and helpful for some people, especially if they have a religious background and are comfortable with it. Just as we don't want people forcing a belief system on us, we don't want to force a lack of a belief system on someone who might be open to one. In this day and age, with non-believers being a fast-growing population, it's likely you'll be able to find someone in any given meeting that is looking for the rational approach that you have to offer. There's no need to push it on people not actively seeking it.

I'll get into other ways to be of service later, but for now, let's assume you've chosen to work with an individual who is coming to meetings and seeking recovery, yet doesn't seem particularly fond of the God thing. The traditional 12-stepping method is quite good. The idea is to initially help the individual feel heard and welcome. A great way to do this is to share some personal stories about how addiction affected you. What was it like to feel stuck in a cycle that you couldn't break out of? How many times did you try to stop unsuccessfully? What did those attempts look like? What were some "war stories" about the more dramatic and humiliating experiences you had?

Talking about this can really help a newcomer feel at home and understood. Once they understand that you "get it." The goal is to then demonstrate to them how you improved your life and got better. Unless you are a therapist, I'd suggest simply sticking with showing them this book and precisely how you went through the steps. Guide them through it using the knowledge that you've gained. This shouldn't be an excruciatingly long process. Encourage the individual to work the steps thoroughly but steadily. If he or she decides to stop or seems resistant, explore why and share any experiences you've had feeling scared or reluctant to do the step work.

Remember that, as a sponsor, your role is not professional advice-giver or amateur therapist. Your goal is to show someone who is suffering precisely how you improved your life and to hold them accountable. End of story. Unless you have been trained specifically to help people through relational or psychological issues, you are in no place to be providing therapy. I'm stern about this rule because I've seen far too many sponsors become arrogant in their position of power and feel as though it is their place to become a life coach and wellness guru. Working these steps and getting sober does not automatically make you a guru of anything other than your personal experience getting sober with the steps. Stick with that and you'll be of great help to someone who is ready to receive your guidance. Go beyond that, and you may do real harm.

It is almost certain that you will eventually come across someone in the 12-step world who is also suffering from some kind of mental health condition. In fact, I would say this is the rule rather than the exception. I have yet to meet anyone with a substance abuse problem or a behavioral addiction that is not also struggling with at least a mild mental health condition. If this is the case, you have one job and one job only: encourage the person to seek professional help. Co-occurring disorders (mental health conditions that exist alongside addiction) are incredibly complex and require the work of a specialist. You can still do this step work with them, but you can't try to get involved in their mental health condition. Conditions such as (but not limited to) PTSD, bipolar disorder, major depressive disorder, panic disorder, schizophrenia, OCD, and personality disorders are far beyond the scope of the steps. If you feel someone's mental health condition is getting in the way of them being able to do the step work as outlined in this book, I beg of you to encourage them to find professional help. You can help them find it if they are not capable themselves.

If you don't want to sponsor someone, I would suggest challenging yourself to at least try being a temporary sponsor. That is, you sponsor someone for a short period of time until they find someone more experienced to ask to sponsor them. If you still believe you don't have the skillset to be an effective sponsor, it's necessary to find some way to regularly be of service. It doesn't have to consume your life, but it should be something that you do at least once or twice a week to help others or contribute to the world in a meaningful way. Donating money or goods is not enough. You need to take specific actions to improve the lives of others. Volunteering, getting a part-time job in a helping field, and being actively involved with newcomers at meetings are all potential options.

Working in the field of recovery is an option, but it needs to be said that this is not a good fit for everyone. Depending on the kind of work you're doing, spending day after day working in addiction treatment can actually hinder your own recovery. You'll often be stuck trying to help people that don't want it and who are in the worst part of their addiction. Many of them have been pushed into treatment by well-meaning loved ones or the legal system. This kind of work is exhausting, sometimes thankless, and isn't always conducive to the kind of connection and fulfillment that this step is meant to help you experience. I work in a helping profession, but I try to limit the work that I do with active addicts. It's not that I don't want to help them, it's about knowing what I can take on while still maintaining my sanity. Full-time work with active addicts is incredibly taxing and a very different experience than working with a few willing addicts who are active in their recovery and willing to change. Of course, this isn't the case in every kind of addiction work, but it is a common experience. If you do decide to take on this kind of work, make sure you put that much more effort into surrounding yourself with healthy people who support your recovery.

Putting it All Together

If the idea of maintaining a lifestyle like this feels overwhelming, I completely understand. When thinking about all of these daily practices you've committed to engaging in, it may seem hard to believe you'll have any free time to enjoy the fruits of your labor. While this fear is understandable, it's unfounded. Let's think of all the things you'll be aiming to practice daily:

Activity	Time Taken
Nurturing our goal traits through positive behaviors (step seven)	Approximately five minutes a day at most. Most of these behaviors can be woven into your daily life. No need to carve out much extra time for them.
Making amends when we are wrong and staying mindful of our behavior through regular reflection (step ten)	One or two minutes, one-to-three times per day. Occasionally longer if you have a particularly big amends you need to make. Reflection should only take a minute here and there. This isn't a huge meditation, just a brief reflection.
Meditating (step eleven)	Anywhere from 5-20 minutes per day. More if you want. Try to increase over time.
Being of service to someone in need (step	This is more complicated and depends on what you're doing. Things like volunteering can take several hours a

twelve)	week while taking a commitment at a meeting you already attend technically requires no extra time. Pick something that you can do but still allows you time to live your life.

Looking at this list, you'll see that the amount of total time needed to work the steps daily is not terribly demanding. For most people, this is time you probably would have otherwise spent being idle or doing something destructive. As I said earlier, the step work is not a miracle. Spending an hour a day doing step work is great, but if the other 23 hours of the day are spent sleeping and watching TV, it's only going to go so far. We need more in our lives if we want to be truly happy and balanced. I'll get to that in chapter six.

By the time you've turned this into a routine, the time spent on it will seem like nothing. In the grand scheme of things, it's a miniscule amount of time that results in real, measurable changes in our behavior and overall quality of life. If it still seems like too much, start small. Meditate for five minutes in the morning, call a newcomer for five minutes, then go through your day occasionally practicing your goal traits and reflecting every few hours. Some days are busier than others, and that's fine. Just be conscious of any desire to get lazy and "coast" along in your recovery. Yes, things will probably get easier as you're sober longer, but that does not mean you should be complacent. There will always be days that test your recovery foundation. If you ever feel yourself slipping back into old ways, up your game and do a little more of everything we've discussed thus far.

Complacency is a common struggle people experience in the maintenance stage of their recovery. It's very easy to get used to this new level of mental stability and forget what got you into recovery in the first place. Be on the lookout for that. If you start to lose motivation to meditate, help others, practice building your goal traits, or do a daily reflection, make an effort to get back in touch with the "why" that got you into recovery. It may be worth it to go back to step one for a bit and remind yourself of the pain and helplessness that motivated you to start on this path. But don't beat yourself up. It's human nature to take things for granted, which is why we have to practice doing the opposite. Working with others is a great way to remind yourself of where you can potentially end up if you don't stay the course.

Acknowledging the fact that we will experience ups and downs is an important part of having a healthy, realistic mindset throughout this process. Nobody stays perfectly stable in their program all the time no matter what. Everyone experiences times when they feel strong in their recovery and times when they feel weak. Unfortunately, it's often difficult to see this ourselves. Doing step ten and practicing meditation helps greatly, but ultimately the best way to know if we're slipping back into old ways is through feedback from our friends and family. This is another reason why social support is so important. We all have blind spots. It's possible, and common, for people to be caught off guard by their re-emerging unhealthy behaviors. If you have a good support network, they can often call you out on your backsliding before it gets too damaging.

If you notice yourself becoming more irritable, judgmental, selfish, anxious, and unhappy, don't waste your time hoping that it will go away on its own. Nipping a backslide in the bud is much easier than trying to repair the damage after an extended period of acting out due to poor recovery maintenance. Get in touch with your support system, be of service, go to a meeting, practice your goal traits, or all of the above. It's not worth it to risk the potential devastation of losing your grip on recovery. When people occasionally revert back to unhealthy behaviors, we call it a lapse. When this turns into a full resurgence of old, unhealthy patterns, we call it a relapse[15].

CHAPTER FIVE
RELAPSE

How Relapse Happens

Relapse is something that nobody in recovery plans on. Unfortunately, it can happen. Some people manage to make it the rest of their lives without a relapse, while others relapse often and are sometimes referred to as "chronic relapsers." Relapse is more than a lapse, which is generally defined as a brief recurrence of unhealthy behavior. Relapse is a full-on dive back into destructive patterns after a period of attempting to abstain from them. A relapse is when an alcoholic buys a bottle and has no intention of drinking it like a civilized person. It's when a compulsive overeater stops calling his sponsor or going to meetings, buys a load of high-reward foods, and binges for days, weeks, months, or the rest of his life. Relapse is serious business, and it's worth doing anything you can to prevent it.

Relapse is not an event; it's a process. It doesn't start with full engagement in unhealthy behaviors, it ends up there after a series of subtler changes. For example, a relapse may start simply by getting a new job and getting so invested in it that you majorly cut back on your maintenance behaviors. This leads to a lack of self-care and stability, an increase in unmanaged emotions, and eventually a resurgence of unhealthy coping behaviors. This process can take days or even years. Sometimes it happens quickly, and sometimes it happens so slowly it's hard to notice. Having regular contact with your support network can be an effective strategy for catching relapse in its early stages.

Complacency is something we have to be increasingly

careful of as we progress in our recovery. It's very easy to feel stable after building your recovery lifestyle and fall under the impression that you're "cured." For one, it's impossible to be cured, because you don't have some bacterial infection or fungus that can be eradicated. You have a series of mental and behavioral patterns that are deeply ingrained in your brain. Unless you discover some way to completely remove part of your conditioning, these patterns will always be with you on some level. Anyone, addict or not, is capable of regressing into old behaviors when the going gets tough. Sure, you can develop new patterns that become your default, but that doesn't mean the old ones vanish from existence. Remember that we are a combination of every person we've ever been.

Confidence is not complacency. It's perfectly fine (and helpful, in my opinion) to be confident in your ability to live a healthy, sober life. Confidence is empowering and encourages us to continue on a given path. Complacency is arrogance, which discourages us from continuing on a given path. If I'm a confident football player, I'm going to continue practicing, training, and honing my skills. If I'm complacent, I'm going to stop practicing and settle for my current level of skill. I won't push myself or try to improve. The distinction between the two is subtle but each one has entirely different consequences. If you sense yourself becoming complacent or lazy, it's helpful to have a safety plan in place that utilizes various relapse prevention tools.

Relapse Prevention Tools

The best way to deal with relapse is to prevent it, and the best way to prevent relapse is to stay consistent in your recovery-oriented behaviors, including step work, self-care, and social interaction. Nevertheless, it's unrealistic to think that we won't experience fluctuations in our life that impact how able we are to maintain certain behaviors. For example, you may move, get married, get a new job, have a child (or six), get ill, retire, etc. When this happens, you can do your best to stay on track, but it may not always be possible. In this case, it's important to have some regular checks and balances in your life that get you back on track when things start to get shaky.

Accountability to Others

Let your friends and family know that you are open to being called out if you start reverting back to old behaviors. It's not their responsibility to keep you sober, but it's worth it to let them know you're open to feedback if they want to provide it. As stated earlier, we are often the last ones to notice our descent into old behavior patterns. Having friends and family who keep you honest is an invaluable tool. Members of 12-step programs are obviously great for this, but be aware that some of the more dogmatic members are likely to approach this in a very black-and-white manner, especially if they don't know you well. For example, it's not uncommon for the devout 12-steppers to interpret *any* reduction in meetings as a downward spiral into relapse. I don't think this is necessarily the case. While less time at meetings certainly can be a sign of potential relapse, it is perfectly possible for a person to attend fewer meetings and still fully engage in a recovery lifestyle.

Meetings are one of many possible components of a successful recovery program. Don't let scare tactics keep you from making changes that may be necessary to accommodate other areas of your life such as work or family. That being said, be sure to be brutally honest with yourself about your *overall* recovery-supporting behaviors. If you drop a meeting, what are you replacing it with? It's easy to slowly trim things out of your program over time and wake up one day realizing you haven't done anything to improve your recovery in ages. When this happens under our noses, we are begging for one crappy day to send us into a relapse. If you aren't great about being honest with yourself about these kinds of things, make sure you remain in regular contact with your sponsor, therapist, or other members of your support group.

The Personal Craziness Index (PCI)

A valuable tool for keeping track of how solid you are in your recovery is one that was developed by Dr. Patrick Carnes, one of the world's leading experts on recovery from sex addiction. It's called the Personal Craziness Index (PCI)[16], and the name pretty much speaks for itself. It's a method of regularly keeping tabs on seven core areas of your life that can gauge how well you're doing in your recovery. This tool, while created by a clinician whose focus is sex addiction, is useful to anyone who doesn't take perfect care of themselves all the time (that's everyone).

The basic concept is to pick seven out of ten lifestyle components that are a good measure of how solid your recovery is. Categories include physical health, social interactions, and work life to name a few. In each category, list three behaviors that would indicate that this part of your life is suffering. For example, you might list "working too many hours" under the "work life" category. At the end of each day, go through your list and tally up how many of the seven categories contain at least one of the problem behaviors. The highest score you can get is seven, and the lowest is zero. The higher the number, the weaker your foundation in recovery, and thus the more at risk you are of relapse. The lower, the better. If you notice a high number in one category, it's time to make a change.

I'm not going to give a detailed description of how to do a PCI because that has already been documented in several places in a more thorough manner than I'd be able to include here. I'd highly recommend taking a look at Dr. Carnes' book, *A Gentle Path Through the Twelve Steps*. Otherwise, you can just Google "personal craziness index PDF" and you'll more than likely come across a few different worksheets that guide you through the process. It is often recommended that this tool be used for a 12-week period when you are suspecting a backslide. I see no problem with making it a nightly routine and just continually keeping track of your recovery.

Cutting Out Toxic People, Places and Things

Especially in early recovery, there is a lot to be said for simply getting the heck away from people, places, or situations that are not conducive to your continued recovery. If you're a recovering alcoholic, I'm not going to tell you that you can never go to a bar if, for example, a close friend is having a birthday party there. Having said that, if you are not

100% sure that you are stable and supported in your sobriety, *don't go to bars*. If there's a social engagement somewhere that isn't safe for you, it's OK to say, "no." You don't have to explain yourself or justify your reasons for not going. You can simply say you aren't able to go, and that is the truth if you are feeling at all unstable in your recovery.

Similarly, cut off contact with people that you know are not going to support you in your current recovery lifestyle. I understand that cutting people off entirely feels drastic, but when it comes to our sobriety and mental health, it's often absolutely necessary. Delete your old party friends out of your phone, stop hanging out with co-workers that engage in unhealthy behavior, and don't go to places that give you the urge to use such as clubs, sporting events, fancy restaurants, or whatever. Everyone's triggers (events that spark an urge to engage in addictive behaviors) are personal to them. Determine what yours are and stay away. Again, this will be less necessary when you are relatively secure in your recovery, but for the times when stress is high and your relapse risk is elevated, go back to the basics and keep yourself away from anything that pushes you closer to your pre-recovery lifestyle.

Final Thoughts

Despite your best efforts, it's possible you will experience a relapse. Folks with behavioral addictions seem to be particularly prone to it. It's very common, for example, for compulsive overeaters to occasionally slip into a period of eating outside of their food plan or for sex addicts to give into temptation and look at porn. Why behavioral addicts seem to relapse more is a question I don't have the answer to. I suspect it has to do with the fact that most behavioral addictions require you to walk a fine line of balance, which is more complicated and difficult than complete abstinence. Sobriety from alcohol is straightforward: don't drink alcohol. Sobriety from compulsive overeating, on the other hand, is far more nuanced.

If you experience a relapse, do not beat yourself up. Shame and despair only saps motivation and convinces you that you deserve to be unhappy. Instead, forgive yourself, look at what went wrong, get honest, and take the steps necessary to get back on the proverbial horse. Ask yourself some difficult but important questions. What were you missing in your recovery program? What vices or unhealthy habits were you holding on to? Where were you not taking care of yourself? What new sources of stress entered into your life? Where did your thinking get distorted? Did you convince yourself you might not really be an addict? Did you start to get jealous of people who could drink and use moderately? Did you begin to grow resentful and feel like you were missing out on aspects of life that others get to enjoy? Look at what went wrong, adjust accordingly, and try again. Every attempt at sobriety is another chance to succeed.

CHAPTER SIX
WHAT THE STEPS MISS

As I've mentioned a few times already, the steps are not everything. There's quite a bit that the steps miss when it comes to a complete, well-rounded recovery lifestyle that is fulfilling and sustainable. In this chapter, I'll be highlighting several areas of recovery that I believe the steps do not adequately address. Each section of the chapter will cover a specific component of a complete recovery lifestyle as well as some general guidance for how to ensure that you are incorporating it into your life on a regular basis. Keep in mind that each section could be its own book, so this is not going to be a complete guide. If anything, it can help you determine what your recovery might be missing and point you in the direction of your next source of recovery knowledge.

Nothing covered in this chapter is meant to be a replacement for the steps. I do believe that the work done in the 12 steps is crucial and a well-designed guide to building a solid foundation of recovery. Instead, everything mentioned in this chapter is intended to simply fill in the holes in your recovery that may be left by limiting your recovery to the 12 steps alone. Although none of this is a replacement for the steps, they are equally (and in some cases more) important than the steps themselves. I have yet to meet someone who really has the kind recovery I want who is also missing any of the components discussed here.

Physical Health

We are machines that have evolved to move. A lot. On top of that, the mind does not exist in a vaccuum; it is connected to the body, and the body to it. I don't mean this in some kind of metaphysical, spiritual sense. I mean it quite literally. Every part of our body is affected by every other part. We are a complete system, and all components need to be cared for if we are to operate at our best. For this reason, I am continually blown away by the lack of emphasis on physical health in the 12-step program.

One of the initial things I noticed when arriving at my first meeting was the cloud of cigarette smoke and the wafting aroma of freshly-brewed coffee and pastries. Don't get me wrong, I understand why. People are desperate to get sober when they start going to meetings, so smoking a cigarette and eating a donut is pretty mild in comparison to the alternative. That being said, it sent me a pretty clear message that physical fitness is very low on the priority list when it comes to what the 12-step program values. Sure, there are people in the 12-step world who have caught on and realize the importance of staying fit, but they most probably didn't learn it from the program itself.

It's conceivable that steps six and seven could indirectly address the topic of physical health. Laziness and gluttony might be considered character defects that can be countered through regular exercise and proper diet. I still find this to be woefully insufficient. Rather than being something that people might think to include in their program, it should be emphasized as a crucial component of true recovery. The changes I've seen in clients who start taking care of their bodies is glaring. It's impossible not to notice their increased confidence, improved mental clarity, and positive shift in attitude. Unfortunately, the steps as they are now basically ignore physical health, which is a huge oversight.

No matter what the presenting problem, when a client walks into my office, I do not end the first session without asking some very basic questions about self-care, the first of which is almost always about exercise. Exercise is an absolutely essential part of *life*, let alone recovery. Exercise increases self-confidence, boosts production of "feel-good" neurotransmitters in our brain, relieves stress, improves cognitive functioning, combats anxiety, helps alleviate depression, promotes healthy sleep, and so on[17]. It's not an exaggeration to say that we are abusing our bodies if we aren't exercising. Lack of exercise has been touted by some as being as detrimental to your overall health as smoking. It is considered a substantial factor in the development of multiple chronic illnesses including cancer[18].

So, do you need to become a gym rat to stay sober? Obviously not. It probably won't hurt, but we're looking for balance. For starters, just stand up and go for a walk every day. Intensity is important, so if you can make it a brisk walk that elevates your heart rate and even gets you sweating a little, that's great. Working out in the afternoon or evening is better than nothing, but my personal experience has been that exercising in the morning is a phenomenal way to start your daily routine and sets the tone for the entire day. Tomorrow, set your alarm for 30 minutes earlier than usual, get up, go for a brisk walk for 20–30 minutes, and then carry on about your usual routine. Watch how different you feel throughout the day. Couple this with meditation and you're golden.

Aim for at least 30 minutes of physical activity three days per week. The more the merrier up to a point. It's not uncommon for folks with addictive tendencies to get obsessive about exercise and run themselves into the ground. Start slow. Walking briskly is perfectly fine. Once you feel like that is no longer cutting it, try something more intense. Obviously, consult with your doctor before beginning any physical exercise regimen. Certain populations need to be more careful than others when it comes to starting a new exercise routine.

One of the most popular forms of exercise is aerobic exercise. Aerobic exercise refers to any exercise that primarily utilizes the aerobic energy system of our bodies, that is, the system that uses oxygen as its chief source of fuel[19]. This is the "low and slow" exercise that many people loathe due its boring nature. Jogging, hiking, and walking are all classic examples. Although often boring, aerobic exercise can be meditative and relaxing. It's a great way to spend some time improving your physical fitness and mental fitness simultaneously. On a day when you're feeling overwhelmed or stressed, try some mindful jogging. For each step you take, try to notice your foot hitting the ground and focus exclusively on that sensation. It's not easy, but it can do wonders for an overactive brain.

Although aerobic exercise is great, don't neglect the weights. Strength training has its own set of incredible benefits, not limited to its ability to reduce symptoms of anxiety[20]. In addition, I have seen strength training lead to significant increases in a person's sense of self-sufficiency, confidence, and self-esteem. In my practice, I've watched strength training specifically improve the lives of addicts, insecure teens and young adults, victims of trauma and abuse, and people suffering from mild-to-moderate depression. I'm not saying it cures any mental health condition, but it seems to improve nearly all of them. If you've never lifted a weight before, it's worth spending a few bucks on a book or a good personal trainer to get you familiar with resistance training. It can be very intimidating at first, but once you get the hang of it, you'll realize it's nothing to be afraid of. The feeling of getting stronger is one of the most rewarding experiences an individual can have. And I am *absolutely* including women in everything I just said. No, you won't get "bulky." You'll get lean, confident, strong, and awesome.

You don't even need a gym membership to start. Bodyweight exercises are fantastic and can be modified to almost any level of difficulty. Some fitness enthusiasts focus exclusively on bodyweight exercise and their results are phenomenal. You can make extraordinary progress with nothing more than a floor. The only piece of equipment you'd probably want to buy is a pull-up bar. Start with the kind that you can mount in your doorway. Good pulling exercises are hard to do at home otherwise. If you're looking for more detailed information on strength training, I'd suggest looking at the *New Rules of Lifting* series by Lou Schuler and Alwyn Cosgrove. These books are excellent for beginners who want a basic understanding of strength training and have no idea where to start.

Regardless of what you decide to do, remember that you *have to* move. It is absolutely mandatory. I know I sound like a broken record, but I cannot stress enough how much your life will improve if you go from sedentary to active. When you start becoming physically active, everything gets better, and that's not an exaggeration. Just start slow, listen to your body, consult with a physician first, and you'll be fine. No matter your initial fitness level or physical limitations, there is always something that you can do to add a little more movement to your daily life, and it's absolutely worth it.

Along with exercise, we have to fuel our bodies properly. Proper nutrition is critical if we want to feel our best. Although high-quality studies on nutrition are exceptionally hard to construct, the scientific literature we do have suggests that nutrition can play a key role in our mood and possibly even reduce the risk of certain mental health conditions like depression[21]. While it most likely isn't a "cure" for mental health conditions, that seems to be the case for any single approach. We aren't trying to find the magic solution to our problems. Instead, we are amassing an arsenal of tools and habits that will have a collective impact on our overall wellness and hopefully remove our compulsive need to self-soothe through unhealthy means.

Remember that our addictive behaviors are not the problem, they are a temporary, but self-destructive solution to a deeper problem. Suboptimal mental health contributes to our desire to engage in addictive behavior, and proper nutrition is one of the many things that can improve mental health. So, while there is no "proof" that nutrition alone can revolutionize your mental health, there is certainly evidence to suggest that, when included as a component of a complete recovery lifestyle, it can help substantially. There's no need to get extreme and become a raw vegan who only eats local produce while barefoot. Start by incorporating more plant-based foods into your diet. Research suggests that the more we lean towards a healthy diet that reduces inflammation and improves the presence of helpful gut bacteria, the lower our risk for many physical and mental health conditions[22].

There are as many different diets as there are books and articles on nutrition. I'm not going to begin to try and dig through all the science and break down how you should eat. People much smarter and more educated than myself have been studying this stuff for decades and still haven't gotten to the bottom of it. Diet is not a simple subject by any means. Regardless, you can educate yourself, talk to a doctor or nutritionist, and try different styles of eating to see what helps you feel the best. Everyone is going to have an opinion about which diet is best for you. Try some things out, read the information that's available, and experiment until you feel like you've found something that works for you. You may not be an expert on nutrition, but you're the expert on how you feel. Listen to your body and follow its lead.

Last but not least, *sleep*. Please sleep. For some reason or another, it has become a mark of success to be constantly sleep-deprived. It's not a mark of success. It's a mark of poor self-care and diminished cognitive abilities (for those who are sleep-deprived, that's a fancy way of saying you're less good at thinking.) Seriously, though, sleep is critical for optimal mood regulation, impulse control, and cognition[23]. Just because some look like they can get away with constant sleep deprivation doesn't mean they can. Arnold Schwarzenegger, one of the hardest working, most successful human beings on the planet famously said that people who sleep eight or nine hours should instead sleep six hours and just "sleep faster" in order to maximize productivity. As much as I admire Arnie, that is dangerous advice. Nothing is worth compromising your sleep.

The processes that occur while we sleep are fascinatingly complex and could only be explained fully in another book. Luckily, a few have already been written. I'd highly suggest reading *Why We Sleep* by Dr. Matthew Walker. It will provide you with all the information you could want regarding what happens during sleep and why sleep is essential. In the meantime, just know that it's non-negotiable. You need to be sleeping as close to eight hours a night as possible. Some people need more.

In order to make sure we get enough sleep, we first have to make sure we *can* sleep. Unfortunately, many people struggle with sleep problems or insomnia. If you're one of these people, it's worth paying attention to your sleep hygiene, which is essentially the sum of the behaviors you engage in that affect your ability to sleep at the end of the day[24]. Proper sleep hygiene consists of multiple small but effective habits, such as:

- **Exercise** – Exercising during the day has been shown to improve amount and quality of sleep. Some people report that exercising too close to bedtime can hinder sleep, so find what works for you.
- **Routine** – Having a bedtime routine isn't just for infants and toddlers. We can all benefit from a few "winding down" habits at the end of the day such as taking a warm bath, dimming the lights and reading, listening to relaxing music, etc.
- **Light** – Research has shown that blue light interferes with our brain's production of melatonin, a necessary hormone that promotes sleep[25]. All of our electronic devices including phones, TVs, tablets, and computer monitors emit a significant amount of blue light. Try turning off all electronics an hour or so before you'd like to sleep and see how you feel.
- **Relaxation** – Relaxation exercises such as meditation, deep breathing, and visualization can all improve

sleep.

- **Keeping the bedroom sacred** – Some people like to do work in bed. Some experts believe that this can create a negative association between stress and being in bed. The bedroom should ideally be only for sleeping and sex.
- **Trying less** – Are you familiar with the experience of shutting your eyes and "trying" so hard to sleep that you just increase your stress and end up counting down the hours you have left before you need to wake up? Instead, try sleeping for 20 minutes. If you don't fall asleep, get up, go to another room, and read or meditate for 20 minutes. Afterwards, try to sleep again. Rinse and repeat.
- **Avoid stimulants** – Try not to consume any caffeine or nicotine too close to your bedtime. Caffeine should be avoided after about noon if you have trouble sleeping or are particularly sensitive to it. Nicotine is also an incredibly powerful stimulant, which should be avoided for a litany of reasons. Don't smoke any meth either.
- **White noise –** Try using some white noise to help you sleep. A common source of white noise is a loud fan, but you can also buy specific devices that either play white noise on a speaker or generate real white noise. The white noise generators (Marpac is one of the most well-known brands) are more expensive, but the sound is much more pleasant and there are no audio loops that obsessive people like myself can get hung up on.

None of these methods have irrefutable scientific evidence to support their efficacy. However, as I've said a few times, I'm a fan of what works. Try these out and see if they help. If not, it may be worthwhile to contact a sleep specialist. Medication is an option, but that can be an *extremely* slippery slope for anyone, and an especially slippery slope for a recovering addict or alcoholic. If you go to a doctor to seek medication as a last resort for sleeplessness, make sure to let him or her know that you have a history of addiction or compulsive behaviors. Doctors don't always do a thorough assessment before prescribing potentially habit-forming drugs.

Communication

Communication is quite literally the only way we can connect with others. Whether it be verbal or non-verbal, there's no way to interact with another human being without utilizing some form of communication. So why are we often so bad at it? Interpersonal communication is something that I believe should be taught in schools. Ideally, our parents and caregivers teach it to us, but that often doesn't happen. Instead, we have to figure it out ourselves by fumbling through our relationships, and we often miss a lot of key lessons. The results of this are devastating. Poor communicators often become anxious, depressed, avoided by peers, misunderstood, and lonely. I have yet to meet an active addict who isn't struggling in some area of communication. This section of the book will be a crash course, but keep in mind that there is a ton to learn about the many aspects of communication, and it's worth learning about. The benefits are significant.

When I was in inpatient rehab, there was a fellow patient, we'll call him "Joe," who regularly got on my nerves. He wasn't overtly rude or unkind, he was just a little socially unaware. He would sometimes joke about people inappropriately and use a sarcastic tone that was abrasive and difficult to listen to. I truly believe he had no ill intentions. He just didn't realize the impact his actions had on others. One weekend, all of the patients and a few of the facility's therapists got together for an outing—kind of like a field trip for a bunch of fidgety addicts trying to get sober. While on the van headed to our location, Joe was acting particularly obnoxious and made some jokes about me that I wasn't in the mood for. My therapist was in the van with us and saw me stewing in silence. I had previously expressed to her in private that Joe got on my nerves, so she knew what I was frustrated about. In that moment, she plainly asked, "Jeff, do you need to tell Joe something?"

I sat there, puzzled. I didn't even realize I *could* say

something. I thought the only way to deal with someone treating you unfavorably was to ignore them and hope the behavior stopped. I was under the impression that speaking up and asking for what I wanted would make me appear whiny, weak, or needy. I decided to put trust in my therapist and follow her prompt. I mustered all the courage I could and simply said, "Joe, please stop."

"Stop what?" Joe asked.

"You keep making jokes at my expense. I don't appreciate it. Please stop," I replied with a bit more confidence.

"Oh, Sorry," Joe responded.

And that was it. The issue was resolved for that moment. My therapist looked at me with a smirk and asked, "Was that so hard?" Well, Yes! It was hard. It was new and scary. I didn't even know it was OK to say things like that, but I took the chance and it paid off. I asked for what I needed and got it. Nobody criticized me and Joe didn't laugh or retaliate. I saved myself so much resentment and frustration just by taking the time to communicate what I was experiencing. This incident was the first time, at 22 years old, that I learned I had a voice, and that I deserved to be heard.

Since then, I have continually practiced direct, assertive communication. Sometimes it works out as well as it did with Joe, and often it doesn't. Either way, the situation ends with me feeling confident that I've said what I needed to say. I'm not bottling up my feelings and holding on to resentments. I speak my mind respectfully but firmly. Sometimes I get what I need and sometimes I don't. When I don't, it gives me good information about the kind of relationship I want to have with the person who isn't willing to respect my needs and boundaries. Since learning how to speak up for myself, I have had significant improvements in my relationships, self-confidence, and anxiety level. When it comes to stress and anxiety, skilled communication is not only a good tool, it's a necessary part of treatment.

All communication falls into four basic categories:

- Passive – Not saying anything. Allowing

mistreatment. Ignoring a problem and hoping it goes away. Passive communication often requires us to deny or ignore our own needs.

- Aggressive – Violence, verbal abuse, intimidation. Aggression is sometimes effective in the short-term, but generally pushes people away. It is toxic to relationships and can get you in all kinds of legal, personal, and professional trouble.
- Passive-aggressive – Trying to retaliate against someone in an indirect or disingenuous way. It's spitting in someone's food, gossiping, or speaking in a vague manner and "dropping hints" about what you need.
- Assertive – Saying what you need to say with confidence, clarity, and integrity. You don't have to be mean to be assertive, but you don't have to sugar-coat either. It's telling someone to stop when they are crossing a boundary. It's telling your friend how you felt when he was rude to you. It's asking for what you need without guilt or shame.

Based on my definitions, it's probably pretty obvious which one I suggest. In 99 out of 100 cases, assertive communication is the way to go. The only exception is when assertive communication has repeatedly failed, in which case you might have to let the situation go or even become aggressive if your safety is in jeopardy, although those situations are hopefully very rare.

If you want to get better at assertive communication, you need to aspire to communicate assertively every chance you get. If I were to take a guess, I'd say that the average person gets at least 100 different opportunities to practice assertive communication every day. It doesn't have to be during some intense, dramatic interaction. It can be as simple as asking for an extra ketchup packet in the drive-thru. The more you practice during the small interactions, the better you'll get at speaking assertively when it really matters. Just to give you some ideas of what healthy, assertive behavior looks like, below are a few examples of how one might respond to various situations using assertive communication.

Event	Assertive response
Husband doesn't call you after work. He usually does. You grow worried and suspect something might be wrong. Turns out he just forgot.	"When you didn't call me after work, I got really worried. In the future, I'd prefer if you just take a minute to let me know you're on your way home."
Coworker consistently criticizes your work and is not your boss. You grow increasingly angry at him.	"Please stop criticizing my work. I don't appreciate it. If something I'm doing is affecting you negatively, let me know and we can talk about it. Otherwise, I'd prefer to get feedback from my supervisor."
Family wants you to come on an expensive vacation with them. You can't afford it.	"I'd love to go, but we just can't afford this trip right now. I hope you guys have a great time. If you need me to be there, we'll have to wait until I'm in a better position to pay for it."
An acquaintance you barely know asks you if you can do her a big favor that makes you feel uncomfortable.	"No."

One of the best lessons I ever learned is that "no" is a complete sentence. You do not owe anybody an explanation for your boundaries. If it's a family member or someone you're close friends with, it will probably serve your relationship better to explain the circumstances a little, but that's still ultimately up to you and not something that I would consider an obligation.

If you look at the examples above, you'll see that none of the responses include an apology. *You do not have to apologize for having needs.* It's extremely common for people to decline requests by saying something like, "I'm sorry, I can't." If it's something you really wish you could do and are truly sorry you can't, fine, but most of the time it seems people apologize because they somehow feel they're doing something wrong.

It's not wrong to have needs and preferences. Some may argue that you're causing harm by rejecting the needs of others. There's a difference between causing harm and disappointing someone by not living up to their expectations. It's reasonable to do our best to avoid harming others directly, but it's unreasonable to expect yourself to please everyone all the time. As an old 12-step friend of mine would say, "If you aren't disappointing at least one person a day, you aren't taking care of yourself." Obviously, that's a bit hyperbolic, but the spirit of the message is an important one to embrace.

Try not to confuse assertive communication with being rude. There is no shortage of individuals who think they are being assertive by "telling it like it is." Any time somebody gives me that line, I can safely assume they probably mean that they are blunt and don't bother to use a filter. They're the kind of person that thinks telling a co-worker, "you're crap at your job" is assertive. Assertive communication is respectful, not harsh or abrasive. It takes a little bit of effort and finesse to do correctly. The point is to speak in a way that will honest and hopefully respected by others. Insults and tactless criticism is not the same as assertive communication.

The more we communicate openly and honestly, the better. There are times we'll need to use our judgment (such as at our place of employment) and determine how open we should be, but ultimately, nothing seems to warrant secretive, indirect, or dishonest communication. If you strive to be direct and honest in all of your dealings with others, you'll see a major change in your life. Not only will people respect you more, but you'll feel less burdened by having to hold on to secrets and resentments. You'll no longer need to remember to whom you told which lie. You'll be able to speak your truth appropriately in any given situation. Development of this skill has the potential to be nothing short of life-changing.

Fun, Hobbies, and Communities

There's one line in the Big Book of Alcoholics Anonymous that enters the realm of addressing fun. On page 132, it states, "We absolutely insist on enjoying life." I insist the same thing, but I'd like to elaborate. Fun is not just a pleasant side effect of recovery, it's an essential component of it. Why would we give up something that was providing us so much comfort (drugs, compulsive sex, alcohol, etc.) if there wasn't something equally or more enjoyable we could experience in return? What's the point of getting sober in the first place? Is it to extend our life expectancy so we can gain twenty years of boredom? Of course not. We're getting sober so we can experience the true joy of living rather than clawing at a series of momentary hits of pleasure.

Some people have no problem at all incorporating fun into their lives, but for many of us addicts, we've been in our addictive cycle for so long that we've forgotten what we enjoy. Many addicts had hobbies and pastimes before they started their addictive behavior, but the emotional pull of addiction eventually became stronger than the desire to get out into the world and do something interesting and fulfilling. The path of least resistance was to stay at home or within our close circle of "friends" while getting high and avoiding the harshness of reality. After doing this for a period of time, old hobbies and fun activities are forgotten about. Our life becomes small and we develop a tunnel-vision focus on achieving the next high.

Sometimes, we need to do something that has no purpose other than to be fun. We have an innate need to goof off from time to time and let go of our responsibilities and commitments. Taking a day off of work to do whatever you want, going to a spa and pampering yourself, going to an amusement park, spending time with an old friend, watching an entire trilogy in one sitting, reading comic books, watching live theater, playing a sport, or anything that doesn't require much effort or willpower are all viable options. If you don't feel like you have time to do any of these things, make time. Sometimes, we need to specifically schedule it into our day if we want it to happen. This is especially true for go-getters and type-A personalities who have a hard time slowing down.

Try to do at least one fun thing every day. It doesn't have to be anything more major than playing a video game (as long as that doesn't become its own addiction, but that's another book) or turning on some music and dancing around your room by yourself. Just give yourself an opportunity to take life less seriously. We're only here for a short period of time and life is really scary and weird, so why not step back every once in a while and just play? Your brain will thank you.

I consider hobbies to be a different category than fun. Not that hobbies aren't often fun, but they can also be challenging and mentally demanding. They don't necessarily give you the same kind of pure relaxation that fun does. That being said, there's a lot that hobbies provide that purely fun activities don't. Hobbies generally involve some kind of creativity or productivity. Fishing, painting, woodworking, knitting, sewing, sketching, gardening—all of these activities end with you possessing something you didn't have before, either by making it or gathering it from the outside world, and this can be an incredibly rewarding experience. If you've ever experienced the excitement of eating a new dish that you cooked yourself or stepping back and looking at your first decent painting, you know how fulfilling a hobby can be.

Hobbies don't generally come to us. In our school years, we often develop hobbies because we are at a point in our lives where we are exposed to lots of different things. As time progresses, however, we can get stuck in a rut and stop exploring what the world has to offer. It becomes necessary to make an effort to search for things that interest us. I have gained hobbies in sobriety that I would never have expected I would like. Part of the fun of looking for hobbies is realizing just how many there are. One of the most enjoyable hobbies I picked up during my later sobriety was knife sharpening. Who would think of that off the top of their head as a potential hobby? In order to find these things, you have to search. The Internet is a great resource, though I'd also consider taking some classes at your local community college or anywhere else that offers them. Taking real-life classes out in the world is killing two birds with one stone. You're discovering a hobby and probably also discovering a community of hobbyists.

Belonging to a community is in our blood. We are social creatures and have a fundamental need to interact with other people on a regular basis. It gives us a sense of purpose and comfort when we feel part of something bigger. In addition, chronic isolation is a breeding ground for depression and anxiety, making relapse more likely. I believe the need for community largely accounts for why organized religion is so popular. A place of worship is a meeting place for members of a community who share beliefs and values. It's a very powerful experience and creates a tremendous sense of connectedness and security. In lieu of church, temple, or other places of worship, us addicts have 12-step meetings. Unfortunately, many of those are still too church-like for us. So what do we do?

While having a recovery community is important, we can still benefit greatly from belonging to other communities as well[26]. The best way to find a community to join is to engage in your hobbies and interests and frequent the locations where like-minded people gather. You may consider going to conventions, workshops, classes, or other events that are related to your hobby or area of interest. When you're there, just talk to people. See what people in the community do and how they communicate with each other. Let people know that you're new to the community and are looking for people to connect with. More often than not, members of a community are excited to talk to other people who share their interests.

Online communities are OK, but I'd advise against settling for one instead of a real world community. Interacting online tends to be much less personal. It's better than nothing, but it can also be an easy way out of challenging yourself to get out into the world and truly connect with other human beings. Sitting down and having a long chat over coffee is not the same as an online forum conversation stretched out over multiple days. If you really want to utilize the Internet, go to a site like meetup.com and use it to search for local meeting places that center around specific interests, hobbies, or demographics. Sometimes, these meet-ups are specifically focused on certain activities, and sometimes they are just opportunities to have unstructured hang-outs with people from a similar demographic (e.g. single parents, atheists, dual-income couples with no kids (a.k.a. "DINKs"), specific age groups, etc.).

The initial stages of joining a community are typically strange and awkward. Unless you happen to be particularly confident and charismatic, new social situations are almost always stressful. Try to remind yourself that the discomfort is a growing pain. It's a sign that you're stepping outside of your comfort zone and therefore expanding it. Be consistent in your pursuit of a community. The more time you spend being part of your community, the more it will begin to feel like home. No matter your interest, there is almost certainly a way to find others who are doing the same thing. This will obviously be easier in more populated areas. If you live in a small town or rural area, don't give up if you can't find a community based around your hobby or interest. It might be a sign that you need to start one yourself. Ultimately, the Internet is always an option if nothing else is available.

EPILOGUE

In roughly half of the world's nations, atheists, agnostics, and religiously unaffiliated people make up the second-largest "religious group" (a misnomer since atheism isn't a religion) that exists[27]. In addition, the number of atheists and agnostics worldwide continues to grow at an increasing rate[28]. Alcoholics Anonymous and its sibling programs have played a remarkably important role in the recovery of millions and millions of people. Unfortunately, the programs have not evolved much since their inception. The unfortunate consequence of this is that they tend to push away members of the growing non-religious populations of the world. Atheists and agnostics deserve just as much of a chance at recovery as believers do, which is the primary reason why I put this guide together.

I hope that this book provides you with an effective, practical approach to the 12 steps that gives you the opportunity to finally be free of whatever addiction or compulsion has been plaguing you. My wish for you is that you wake up every day feeling free to live your life how you choose, not being beholden to your cravings or urges. If this book helps you accomplish that, then I am thrilled. Ultimately, however, I'm a fan of what works. I only know what I know and have blind spots like any fallible human being. If you feel this approach falls short of meeting your specific needs, please continue on your search until you find something that provides you the peace and freedom you deserve.

Recovery is rarely a linear progression from despair to self-actualization. There are obstacles and setbacks along the way, and the process is unique to every individual. Don't let anyone else tell you what your path to recovery needs to look like. Keep an open mind, continue to learn about the many approaches to self-improvement that are available, and don't give up on yourself. The most important ingredient for recovery is hope and persistence. As long as you continue seeking recovery and trust that you can achieve it, you will. It may happen soon, or it may take some time, but it *will* happen if you continue to lean into the process.

As a self-publishing author, I can't express how grateful I am that you've chosen to read my particular book. There are countless self-help books out there that offer approaches to personal growth that are secular in nature. The fact that you picked mine up (or downloaded it) is appreciated more than you may know. So thank you, thank you, and thank you again.

This book has been rattling around in my head for quite some time. Putting it out into the world has been a scary, but exciting experience. I have a special place in my heart for the 12 step program as well as its community members. Even with all of its dogma and religious tendencies, I'm not sure I'd be alive today without it. It has provided me with structure, guidance, and the opportunity to meet some of the most amazing human beings I've ever known.

I wrote this book *because* of how important the 12 step world is to me. I feel very fortunate that I was able to overlook some of the more challenging aspects of the program early on and stick around long enough to get better. Many people may not have the ability or time to do that, and I feel it's my duty to let those people know that there is indeed an option for them. You do not have to force yourself to believe anything without evidence, nor do you deserve to be judged or shamed for being unwilling to take a leap of faith. It is absolutely possible to thrive in the program without needing to believe in anything supernatural. Practical action, evidence-based trust, and social support are enough.

If you want to help this book reach more people, please tell friends, family, or anyone who needs it that it exists. If you're feeling up to it, please leave an *honest* review for this book on Amazon's website. I always want to hear feedback from my readers and am constantly looking for ways to improve my work. If you'd like to get in touch with me directly, you can email me at jeff@jeffreymunn.com. I hope to hear from you.

May Thor bless you and keep you—until then.

ABOUT THE AUTHOR

Jeffrey Munn is a licensed marriage and family therapist who works in private practice in Valencia, CA. He resides in the same city with his wife and daughter. Jeffrey has spent much of his career teaching educators, clinicians, and parents about substance abuse, how to identify it, and how to find appropriate treatment for it.

NOTES

[1] For the uninitiated, a "sponsor" is a person whom you choose (generally from a meeting you attend) to help guide you through the 12 steps.

[2] Robinson, T. E., & Berridge, K. C. (2000). The psychology and neurobiology of addiction: an incentive–sensitization view. *Addiction*, *95*(8s2), 91-117.

[3] Blanco, C., Moreyra, P., Nunes, E. V., Saiz-Ruiz, J., & Ibanez, A. (2001, July). Pathological gambling: addiction or compulsion?. In Seminars in clinical neuropsychiatry (Vol. 6, No. 3, pp. 167-176).

[4] Dobkin, P. L., Civita, M. D., Paraherakis, A., & Gill, K. (2002). The role of functional social support in treatment retention and outcomes among outpatient adult substance abusers. *Addiction*, *97*(3), 347-356.

[5] Dube, S. R., Felitti, V. J., Dong, M., Chapman, D. P., Giles, W. H., & Anda, R. F. (2003). Childhood abuse, neglect, and household dysfunction and the risk of illicit drug use: the adverse childhood experiences study. *Pediatrics*, *111*(3), 564-572.

[6] Cognitive-behavioral therapy is a type of psychotherapy that focuses on faulty beliefs and thoughts that drive our behavior and influence our emotions.

[7] Hofmann, S. G., Asnaani, A., Vonk, I. J., Sawyer, A. T., & Fang, A. (2012). The efficacy of cognitive behavioral therapy: A review of meta-analyses. *Cognitive therapy and research*, *36*(5), 427-440.

[8] Alcoholics Anonymous. (2001). Alcoholics Anonymous, 4th Edition. New York: A.A. World Services.

[9] Bloom, P. (2016). *Against Empathy: The Case for Rational Compassion.* Harper Collins.

[10] Haney, C. (2003). The psychological impact of incarceration: Implications for post-prison adjustment. *Prisoners once removed: The impact of incarceration and reentry on children, families, and communities*, *33*, 66.

[11] Davis, D. M., & Hayes, J. A. (2011). What are the benefits of mindfulness? A practice review of psychotherapy-related research. *Psychotherapy*, *48*(2), 198.

[12] Shields, G. S., Sazma, M. A., & Yonelinas, A. P. (2016). The effects of acute stress on core executive functions: a meta-analysis and comparison with cortisol. *Neuroscience & Biobehavioral Reviews*, *68*, 651-668.

[13] Wikipedia contributors. (2018, September 12). Fight-or-flight response. In *Wikipedia, The Free Encyclopedia.* Retrieved from https://en.wikipedia.org/w/index.php?title=Fight-or-flight_response&oldid=859140731

[14] Cahn, B. R., & Polich, J. (2013). Meditation states and traits: EEG, ERP, and neuroimaging studies.

[15] Marlatt, G. A. and Donovan, D. M. (2005). *Relapse prevention* (second edition). New York: Guilford.

[16] Carnes, P. (2012). *A gentle path through the twelve steps: The classic guide for all people in the process of recovery*. Hazelden Publishing.

[17] Brown, R. A., Abrantes, A. M., Read, J. P., Marcus, B. H., Jakicic, J., Strong, D. R., ... & Dubreuil, M. E. (2009). Aerobic exercise for alcohol recovery: rationale, program description, and preliminary findings. *Behavior modification*, *33*(2), 220-249.

[18] Booth, F. W., Roberts, C. K., & Laye, M. J. (2012). Lack of exercise is a major cause of chronic diseases. *Comprehensive Physiology*, *2*(2), 1143.

[19] Plowman, S. A., & Smith, D. L. (2013). *Exercise physiology for health fitness and performance*. Lippincott Williams & Wilkins.

[20] Gordon, B. R., McDowell, C. P., Lyons, M., & Herring, M. P. (2017). The effects of resistance exercise training on anxiety: a meta-analysis and meta-regression analysis of randomized controlled trials. *Sports Medicine*, *47*(12), 2521-2532.

[21] Lai, J. S., Hiles, S., Bisquera, A., Hure, A. J., McEvoy, M., & Attia, J. (2013). A systematic review and meta-analysis of dietary patterns and depression in community-dwelling adults–. *The American journal of clinical nutrition*, *99*(1), 181-197.

[22] Selhub, E. (2015). Nutritional psychiatry: your brain on food. Retrieved from

https://www.health.harvard.edu/blog/nutritional-psychiatry-your-brain-on-food-201511168626

[23] Walker, M. P. (2009). The role of sleep in cognition and emotion. *Annals of the New York Academy of Sciences, 1156*(1), 168-197.

[24] Irish, L. A., Kline, C. E., Gunn, H. E., Buysse, D. J., & Hall, M. H. (2015). The role of sleep hygiene in promoting public health: A review of empirical evidence. *Sleep medicine reviews*, *22*, 23-36.

[25] West, K. E., Jablonski, M. R., Warfield, B., Cecil, K. S., James, M., Ayers, M. A., ... & Hanifin, J. P. (2010). Blue light from light-emitting diodes elicits a dose-dependent suppression of melatonin in humans. *Journal of applied physiology*, *110*(3), 619-626.

[26] McGreevey, S. (2011, September 12). *What makes AA work?* Retrieved from https://news.harvard.edu/gazette/story/2011/09/what-makes-aa-work/

[27] Hackett, C., Huynh, T. (2015, June 22). *What is each country's second-largest religious group?* Retrieved from http://www.pewresearch.org/fact-tank/2015/06/22/what-is-each-countrys-largest-religious-group/

[28] Cheyne, J. A. (2009). Atheism rising: The connection between intelligence, science, and the decline of belief. *Skeptic (Altadena, CA)*, *15*(2), 33-38.

Made in the USA
Monee, IL
14 January 2024

51777203R00096